Tupac Behind Bars

Michael Christopher

Tupac Behind Bars

Prende Publishing

Las Vegas ◊ Chicago ◊ Palm Beach

Published in the United States of America by
Histria Books
7181 N. Hualapai Way, Ste. 130-86
Las Vegas, NV 89166 USA
HistriaBooks.com

Prende Publishing is an imprint of Histria Books. Titles published under the imprints of Histria Books are distributed worldwide.

Library of Congress Control Number: 2021952703

ISBN 978-1-59211-137-4 (hardcover)
ISBN 978-1-59211-199-2 (softbound)
ISBN 978-1-59211-266-1 (eBook)

Contents

In Clinton Prison, there are two colors:

He wore Green.

I wore Blue.

This book is based on actual events. The author has tried to the best of his ability to recreate the conversations and memories of incidents as they actually occurred. To provide some privacy for himself, he has written under an alias. In some cases, the individuals are not mentioned by name in the book to protect themselves and their families. The names of some individuals and places have also been changed, as well as identifying characteristics and details such as physical properties, occupations, and or places of residence.

Introduction

Before June 6, 2015, when New York State's largest manhunt ever made national headlines with the escape of two convicted killers from Clinton Correctional facility and made Dannemora a recognizable name, this sleepy little town already had its taste of fame. On March 8, 1995, rapper 2Pac Shakur walked in shackles through the hardened steel gates that led inside the bowels of the hundred and fifty-year-old prison. He served his time there until his release on bail on October 12 of the same year. Little has ever been written about this 2017 Rock-and-Roll inductee's time inside the largest maximum-security prison in New York State or his relationship with security staff and little outside the thirty-foot-high cement walls is known about his days there. My name is Michael Christopher. I was a corrections officer who met Tupac Shakur at the crossroads of his life and perhaps my own in one of New York's most evil places.

Inside Clinton prison, there is an invisible line between inmates and officers like an invisible fence for animals and inmates generally know where this line is. Inside New York State prisons, the inmates usually address officers as, CO (Corrections Officer) or by their last name, sometimes they just use the word officer, and sometimes they use the first initial of the officer's last name like Mr. B or Mr. C., which is more of a slang term. These terms are usually acceptable by most officers; addressing Corrections staff in this way is considered a sign of respect. Inmates are called by their last name, a nickname, and some officers will tell you by pretty much whatever they want to call them but there is a strict rule that inmates never call officers by their first name. Fraternization on this level is always prohibited. The following accounts of the interaction that I had with inmate Shakur are based on facts. The dialogue between Tupac Shakur and I are written to the best of my recollection, including the choice of slang words to describe those events. The use of the word "nigga" was used frequently by Tupac and the use of the racial slur "nigger" was heard occasionally at Clinton by a few officers. To say that all the officers at Clinton in 1995 were prejudice, however, would be an injustice to the professional men and women that worked there.

Much has been said about Tupac over the years since his death in 1996. Time and time again, I have watched and read things about him and I sometimes just start to laugh. Some of the things make me laugh because I can still hear him say them, in my mind, and sometimes I laugh because I know that what is said is just pure excrement from a bull. One of the things that I hear over and over again is how people mispronounce Tupac. It is not 2 pack. It is pronounced 2 like the number and 'poc' like pocket. He hated it when people said 'pack' but over the years, I've heard it said that way by reporters and people interviewed that said they knew him.

Tupac has been recognized as one of the greatest rappers of all time, listed in the Guinness book of world records in 2004 as the highest-selling Rapper artist selling more than 67 million albums worldwide and in 2019 over 75 million. He is also sometimes called the black Elvis. The only Rapper I'm aware of with this moniker because of the arguable speculation that he cheated death, with endless sightings after his demise that continue to this day. He was also a notable poet, songwriter, actor, street thug, gangster, and a convicted criminal. And yes, I admit that his reputation lent himself to be recognized as a thug and a gangster but the man I knew as Pac did not present himself that way to me. I knew a different side. We all have two sides I think, the one everyone thinks they know and recognize and then there is the one that is only seen from within. Tupac was a Yin and a Yang. He had a dark side and he had a side that was like Mercury light. The side I got to see I believe was a real depiction of him stripped of his gold chains and rings; inmates cannot possess gold chains unless they have a religious affiliation and a value of not more than fifty dollars and no rings unless it's a wedding ring of no more than a hundred-dollar value. He also lost his identity as a celebrity. It did not exist in this world that he now lived in and last he was void of any entourage for support or protection. The only protection inside Clinton prison that he was going to get from the state was from the officers that watched him, and the majority of them didn't like him because of his sex crime or the thug life they thought he represented. In the state of New York's eyes, he was just a DIN number 95-A-1140 that identified him as being the one thousandth one hundredth and fortieth inmate that was processed in 1995 and nothing else.

The man I saw five days a week was raw, vulnerable, street smart, humble, funny, and meek. Although, I'm sure that he was frightened too but I don't think I ever met a first-time inmate that wasn't scared in prison but like Mark Twain had once realized and said was — "Courage is resistance to fear, mastery of fear-not absence of fear.

During Tupac's incarceration, I watched him evolve from a man that, by his own admission to me, was quite prejudice and untrusting when I first met him. When he first arrived in Clinton, he once said that he thought people should only marry their own kind. He was careful to say it was only his opinion, but I could tell it was a strong one. But before he left prison, I began to see changes in him. He had built a strong friendship with a white inmate and I believe that he and I had built a mutual respect for each other. It looked to me like he was beginning to judge the person for the truth of what they told him and also what they did and not the color of their skin or even what color shirt they wore on the outside. In prison people lie so much it is hard to tell fact from fiction. Sometimes the line is blurred between the two. Joe (Mad Dog) Sullivan who did time at Clinton was an infamous contract killer for the Westies, an Irish mob out of New York City, credited with disposing of Jimmy Hoffa's body in the book "Contract Killer" in 1993 written by another contract killer "Tony the Greek" A.K.A. Donald Frankos, who also did time at Clinton. Joe Sullivan, or Sullie as he was sometimes called, escaped from Attica prison in 1971. He was the first person to successfully do so from a prison that was thought to be escape-proof. Inmate Sullivan once told me that a lot was written about him, but probably it was ninety-five and five percent. One ratio was truth and the other total bullshit, but only he knew which was which. Mad Dog also once told me how much he liked me, but that if I ever stood between him and a way to escape that he would have to kill me. That was one time I didn't have to ask myself if an inmate was telling the truth.

I want to make it clear that it was evident to me from the beginning when I first met Tupac that he was no saint to be venerated, but I never saw him as the apostle of Satan either. Some inmates, in my opinion, can never be rehabilitated because they lack remorse, a conscience, and the ability to change but for Tupac, I thought that he not only was capable of change but I had witnessed changes in him already and I had no doubt that he could influence others and have a positive impact on them as well. And as the magazine *SWING*, in January 1997, posthumously listed Tupac as one of the most powerful people in their twenties, it appears the masses agreed.

I will always remember his passion, and his inability to totally contain himself when describing his insatiable appetite for life. He saw things not as they are but as he thought they could be, he reminded me very much of the passion that John F. Kennedy displayed when he delivered his famous speech about choosing the task of putting the first man on the moon and how man set their sight on the moon not because it was easy but because it was hard. I believe that Tupac thought he could change the world. But I must admit that when I first met Tupac with his cloak of silent attitude, I had to remind myself of other words of John F. Kennedy that humbly said "Never corner an opponent, and always assist him to save face. Put yourself in his shoes — so as to see things through his eyes. Avoid self-righteousness like the devil — nothing is so self-blinding."

Tupac and I definitely had an unlikely relationship since some of the biggest problems he had in his life he told me had been with authority and with white people and I happened to represent both. This book is dedicated to Tupac's memory in prison. A time I'm sure that, if he had lived, he would have wished the world would forget, not the time he did, because that adds to his gangster credentials, but the crime, with its negative stigma, that he insisted he didn't commit. He stood apart from any another inmate that I've ever known, and I have known thousands before him and thousands after. I did, however, see him as the same as every other human being, no more, no less, like everyone else on this earth, and just as fallible. This human weakness reminded me of Richard Nixon, the only President of the United States ever to resign from office, and who in his final hours as president had reached probably the lowest point in his life but still found the words to warn his fellow man to avoid a similar fate. In his farewell speech just before he boarded Air Force One for the last time, he spoke from his heart and said, "always remember, others may hate you but those who hate you don't win unless you hate them, and then you destroy yourself."

The writing of this book is a culmination of notes and stories that I have told others, and in my mind, I have relived over and over for more than twenty years. The story is not long — short in fact much like the life of Tupac. I must mention that while writing these pages I experienced many odd things. In the beginning, my computer would freeze up and I lost many pages that mysteriously refused to save; I rewrote them. Then my printer refused to print. I kept having glitches with Word pad, the writing program that came with my computer, and I changed it to Microsoft Word. The lights in the room where I wrote would dim and then return to normal. My TV would turn off and come back on by itself. Then it was strange noises that kept coming from the area where my computer is, and while I was typing at my desk, a big sturdy dictionary that always stands under my desk fell, without reason, against my leg as if nudging me. I was trying to tell my family members about the strange things happening. My computer screen had pages of this book displayed while I was talking, and all of a sudden, I couldn't hear the person on the other end. It was silent, but the phone still showed a strong connection. This was a landline. I called them back and asked if they hung up. They told me they could hear me. Then I was away from my home and I was talking on my cell phone to a friend and the same thing happened on that phone. This was the second thing that day. Later, the same day, I was at a gas station pumping gas and the gas pump froze up. I went inside and asked the attendant what was wrong and he said nothing. The pump was showing normal on his computer inside. I said, well come outside and see for yourself. He tried to pump the gas and nothing happened. He said that he has never seen this before. I told him it's weird, isn't it? And he agreed it was very weird. It's been said that things always happen in threes and Tupac and I had talked about the power of the number three.

When I discussed with my wife all the strange things that happened that day, she asked me if I really thought it was him and I insisted it was. She then asked me if maybe Tupac didn't want the book written. I told her not to worry; I believed he is probably trying to tell me not to give up because surely he wouldn't have given up. But I must admit I did wonder if he doesn't like me portraying him as being mortal with common weaknesses shared by all men; capable of tears and the strong desire to be accepted... and to belong. This is something I believe that he would not want anyone to see, that this tough gangster rapper was capable of, outside of his family and trusted friends. But I continued to write about him the way I saw him because I feel his frailties identifies him as being like the rest of us and not just a celebrity wrapped up in his own hype. I am sure that it was Tupac reaching out from wherever he is, and anyone that knew the real Tupac will tell you that he would be the one person who would try to break through from the other side.

The same night after my wife and I spoke about whether or not Tupac was in some way trying to communicate with me I had a dream and, in the dream, I saw a flat-screen TV. It was a blank black screen except for a box in the upper left-hand corner. (On my television, in reality, I have cable with caller ID, and when someone calls their name shows up in a black box in the upper left corner of the screen). This box is what I saw in my dream. The name said Tupac Amaru. I started reading the name and immediately woke up. I told my wife. She listened to me as she always has and hugged me. I didn't really want to tell her because it frightens her but I have always been unable to keep things from her both good and bad; we share everything. It doesn't bother me that it feels as if I have some type of energy with me because for me it gives comfort. I honestly believe that Tupac is somehow, in some form, still with me, even if it's just in my memory or in my dreams.

Clinton

Correctional Facility

Main Street
Dannemora, NY

Chapter I

You're Not in Kansas Anymore

March 8, 1995, will forever be a bullet inoperable in my brain. This day will always, for me, remain a mystery that has left me in a state of introspection; that everything happens for a reason and that my simplest memories will fade with time while Tupac Shakur will forever hang like a flag, half-mast, perpetually in my mind. He was an inmate, yes, but a human too. He was convicted by twelve jurors. He was sentenced and sent to Dannemora to be confined to Clinton Correctional Facility to serve his days inside a single six by eight-foot cell and caged like an animal. My job was to make sure he didn't escape this zoo. I was the Keeper, and he was the Kept. Inside New York State prisons there are two colors:

He wore green. I wore blue.

A draft of twenty or more new inmates arrived at the facility late that afternoon. They were all dressed in the same drab green outfits and were herded like cows down the corridor leading to the gymnasium. They were standing single file, six or seven feet behind a security gate called the "eighty-eight," a common spot for officers to hang out between duties. I remember I was just listening to a couple of officers talk about the usual, who's Buck had more points on its' rack last Deer hunting season, how they couldn't wait for fishing season to go catch some Brook Trout, and how good some cold beer was going to taste after work, when a gruff voice echoed down the hall.

"Listen up convicts! Keep your eyes straight ahead and keep your mouths shut. You're in Clinton now. You're not in Kansas anymore." The escorting officer wrapped his hand tightly around the ribbed rubber grip on his wooden baton, the only protection an officer has inside the walls, as he warned them. Most inmates, if not all, already knew where they were. Clinton Correctional Facility was a place of fear, with a reputation that went back to its beginning in 1845. The officers here are family, literally. Many of the officers had fathers and grandfathers, brothers and sisters, cousins and so on, that had walked the same beat inside the original walls that are part of the history of the Adirondack Mountains in the North Country, more than five hours from New York City. This prison was, and remains, one of the biggest employers in an economically depressed region.

One of the officers standing near me yelled out, loud enough I'm sure for all the inmates lined up to hear him, "Which one of those mutts is that movie star, rapper guy?" Another officer chimed in "that's him there," as he pointed to a young black man

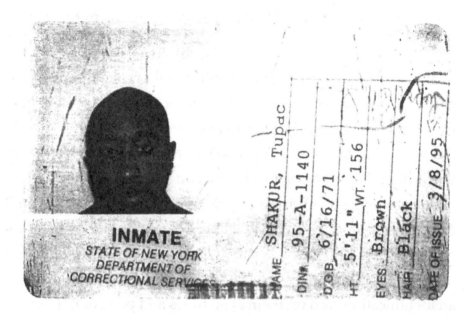

with a slender build just shy of six feet tall, with an almost bald head and really thick eyebrows.

"Looks like another poor dumb nigger to me," the officer that asked replied.

A few of the officers laughed. I did not. Instead, I stood there trying to get a better look at him. To me he didn't look like the rest of the inmates, standing there looking straight ahead, with that look of surrender in their eyes, and fear on their faces. Tupac had a slightly different look like that of shell shock, or maybe culture shock because all of the officers at Clinton in 1995 were white, except one, and his father was white, or maybe because he couldn't believe anyone would call him a "nigger" standing in front of his face.

A few days later, that same officer that had called Tupac "nigger" was in front of his cell with another officer. Guys like him travel in pairs, asking him for an autograph for his wife. He said she was a big fan. Then Tupac asked the officer, "What's your wife's name?" According to what he told me, he wrote — "To (the officer's wife's name), from the richest, smartest, nigger, you'll ever meet — Peace — Tupac Shakur." After he signed an autograph for this guy, the officer then had the balls to give him a direct order to give him his identification card. Inmates must carry an identification card on them at all times and present it upon demand from any officer. Tupac said he gave it to him and the officer smirked at him, looked at the other officer as if to say I told you he was dumb, put it in his pocket, and walked away. The same officer that took Tupac's ID apparently couldn't wait to show it off to anyone that would listen at the bar across from the prison where some of the officers frequently drank beer after work. The word got back to the Superintendent of Clinton that he had it in his possession and was asked to report to his office and return the ID back to the facility, which he did. I don't know what happened in that office, but nothing disciplinary ever happened to this guy. Maybe the facility didn't want the bad press if the word got out that Tupac was having problems with staff.

Tupac would later tell me that story about the officers visiting him at his cell and say, "I recognized that one CO, same KKK mutha' fucker that called me nigger; I know you guys got KKK members up here in the backwoods sittin' on their porches playin' banjos and shit but I didn't say nuthin'. After all, it's your house Mr. C." (He chose to call me by my last name's first initial which I didn't object to). He started to pretend to play the air banjo and making the noises from the song "Dueling Banjos" made famous in the movie Deliverance with Burt Reynolds back in 1972. He was very animated. I knew he was just kidding around, and I thought it was funny. We both started laughing.

This would not be the only incident between corrections officers and Tupac Shakur. A few weeks later a short, chubby, officer with racial biases, that he seemed quite proud of, was accused of bitch slapping Tupac with an open hand slap in the face like a woman would do, on the way back to his cell after a visit. The assault was investigated. The officer officially denied it. I was told at the time by friends of his that he was quite nervous about it, that he might be in serious trouble. The investigation concluded finding nothing to support the allegations, no witnesses, and soon after he was bragging to his clique that he slapped the Rape-o Rapper and said Shakur was no gangster but a punk. The officer became known among his cronies as the Rapper Slapper. Tupac would also tell me about some of this incident after I asked him if it happened. All he said was, "Mr. C., I ain't no snitch, but let's say that little weeble wobble but you don't fall down mutha' fucker hits like a fuckin' bitch. I didn't fight back cause I don't fight with little girls," he laughed.

It's hard to believe that the first time I spoke to Tupac he didn't say two words, just a yes or no response. I have seen enough haters in prison both officers and inmates to recognize someone who is prejudice. He didn't like white people. He had a familiar grimace on his face, and his eyes glared as he stared straight ahead. It was a nonverbal cue, but I knew what it meant. This behavior he exhibited I'd seen hundreds of times during my career as an officer, and it spoke volumes to me. So, I asked him point-blank, "What is your hang-up with me? Is it because I'm white? Or is it because I'm an officer? Or is it both?" He looked at me with a strange and bewildered look. I could tell he was perplexed and after a pause of a few seconds he raised his chin up and asked, "you wanna know?"

"Yeah, I want to know."

"Ok." He got serious; something that I wouldn't ever see from this point forward. "Well, it ain't personal, I don't know you but I have had a lot of bad experiences with whites, stealin' from me in business, police beatin' me, pushing my face into the sidewalk for crossing the street, CO's in here callin' me nigger and most of you whites just tryin' to ruin my life." He reached up with his hand to his mustache and rubbed the hairs newly growing in, probably wondering if he was going to get beat up for saying his piece. After all, it was Clinton.

"Well... inmate Shakur" I looked straight at him into his coffee-colored eyes, "I understand. When I started in Corrections, I worked at Sing Sing and the majority of officers there were black, except for the transient COs, mostly from up North and out West by Attica. My first few days there were rough. The officers from New York City treated me like shit and called me "Frozen Brain" because I lived near Clinton. They used to joke with each other that all the officers from that far North were dumb because our brains were solid ice. I stepped to them one at a time, up close and personal, and asked them why they had a problem with me because I didn't know them and they certainly didn't know me. These officers mostly gave me blank looks and fixed eye stares that seem to last a while but then slowly most changed their attitudes and gave me a chance to prove myself. I guess they didn't expect me to talk to them and really didn't expect me to give a fuck if they talked to me or not. But I did. Soon, they were talking to me, and I felt like I was fitting in. I actually didn't mind working there and most of the officers were pretty good people. So, I hate to burst your bubble, this little world that you live in, but not all of us white people are assholes. I know that not all black people are assholes either, but we both have them though, don't we? I know white guys that are pieces of shit and I bet you know black guys that are pieces of shit too. I'm going to tell you what an old officer with forty years on the job told me, "treat every man the same. They get what they give. Give respect, get respect. Be an asshole and get your ass kicked. He said it wasn't his job to punish anyone. He was no judge. They didn't pay him enough for that shit. He wasn't looking for trouble, but he wasn't running from it either, and I feel the same way. So, if you have a problem with me, be a man and tell me to my face."

A few seconds passed, and I wasn't sure how this was going to play out. Sometimes when an officer calls an inmate out the inmate gets what COs call "froggy" because they leap forward and throw a punch. I cautiously waited for his response. But then I saw a slow smile beginning to grow across Tupac's face. I guess he was sizing me up. Trying to tell if I was "frontin'," something the inmates would say to someone that pretends to be something they aren't. "Cool," Tupac said as he looked straight at me "Okay, I got no problem with you, Mr. Christopher." He shook his head up and down and swung his arm up with his hand open for me to shake. "Hi, my name is Tupac Shakur. I mean," he lowered his voice, "inmate Shakur." He cracked a smile and giggled a little, probably thinking I wouldn't think he was sincere if he laughed. This was the first time I really saw him relax from his tense posture and begin to smile, the way a comedian smiles when they laugh at their own jokes. And I don't remember him losing that signature smile for the rest of the time that I knew him. I must admit, when I saw Tupac, I had no idea who he was other than what the officer said that he was an actor and a rapper. I never heard of him and now for no reason that I can honestly give other than that sometimes you meet someone and you just like them you can't explain it you just do. I found myself wanting to get to know him better. The man, not the celebrity.

It would be many years later that I realized that when I told Tupac that I understood — I did not. It would take a friend of many years to make me see the light about race. My friend is Spanish. Born in Puerto Rico and moved to the Bronx when he was young and later to the North Country. During a conversation one day, I said to him that I never really saw hate or racism here in Upstate New York. He quickly set me straight. He had three daughters and when they were young, they would come home almost daily from school crying uncontrollably because the kids called them hurtful racial names for being different. He said the pain this caused his kids has never gone away. I guess I lived with blinders on. I honestly thought that all people are equal and at the moment I realized that not all people feel the same as me.

But on the day, years ago when I told Tupac that I could relate (I thought I did), and when he reached out his hand, yeah, I shook it. His handshake did take me by surprise though because it was different. It started like a regular formal handshake, which I was used to. But then he pulled back and curled his fingers. I curled mine locking them together then letting go. He came back in with a fist, and I bumped it with my fist, and then he brought his fist up and hammered it down on mine. I then returned with mine and pounded down on his. I imagine that most officers at Clinton would never consider shaking hands with an inmate, and not like this hand shake that was considered black, a street thing, here at Clinton. Most officers wouldn't shake an inmate's hand at all, especially not a black one. I wanted to show him an act of faith to let him know that my word was good. I sort of considered it like a treaty between two different cultures that we could coexist, like the Government's word they gave the Native Americans in the 1800s, except I meant it. From that moment forward we had an understanding that as long as he did what he was supposed to, he would receive respect from me and I expected his respect in return. Even though just the blue color of my officer's shirt in Clinton commanded respect from any inmate there, I preferred that he willingly gave it and not under duress.

Chapter II

The Change

At the time of Tupac Shakur's arrival, I was a Corrections Officer assigned to the school area of a special unit called APPU, the acronym for Assessment and Preparation, Program Unit. This unit houses high-profile inmates that would not be able to survive or be at great risk of being hurt or killed in population. I was the first officer in the school area during the week, and I was the visiting room officer on the weekends. I supervised the visits of both APPU and E-block inmates; the blocks are lettered such as A, B, C, etc. E-block was a protective custody or "PC" unit. Tupac was housing in E-block shortly after he arrived for his safety and the safety of the facility. He had just transferred in from Riker's Island, a city jail that was staffed with a high percentage of black officers, where inmates wait to be sentenced to state time and he had been kept separate from the rest of the inmates while he was temporarily housed there. The State of New York had sent Tupac to Dannemora because of its distance from New York City. He was less likely to get big media attention here in the remote mountains about an hour from the Canadian border; a place with the antiquated nickname 'Little Siberia' for its' subzero winter temperatures. Clinton's administration was afraid of putting a high-profile inmate like him in the general population or "pop" with other inmates that might either love the Rapper for his fame or hate the Rapper for his fame or his affiliation to the East Coast or the West Coast or the Bloods or the Crypts. Any of these scenarios would create chaos inside a Correctional setting.

At no time in Tupac's incarceration was he ever in general population with the average violent inmate. In fact, it was the opposite. He was protected from the moment he was sentenced until his departure from prison. If anything happened to Tupac while housed at Clinton Correctional, this would be a huge liability for the State of New York. And nothing did happen to Tupac physically, sexually, or otherwise, at least not from any other inmate while he was at Clinton. I watched an interview a few years back where someone claimed that Tupac was raped at Clinton. Not true. Rape does occur inside Clinton, of this I have no doubt, as it does, I'm sure, in every prison setting. But what people don't realize is that it's seldom witnessed by any staff and even more seldom reported by the inmate out of fear of their life. With that said, the opposite was true of APPU, which was known for its snitches, and that information would have been like holding the winning lottery numbers. And no one ever tried to cash that ticket.

One of my tasks after visits finished on weekends was to help the other officers strip frisk the inmates and escort them back to their cell blocks. A strip frisk of an inmate is accomplished by taking the inmate to a private location in the visiting room and telling him to remove his clothes down to his undershorts if he's wearing any. Some inmates don't wear underwear and they cut the pockets out of their state pants, which are always the color green, to provide easy access for their visitors to touch their genitals if the opportunity presents itself. The inmate hands his clothes to the officer who frisks them, making sure no contraband is hidden there and then the officer directs the inmate to face him, open his hands, and spread his fingers so that he can see if anything is hidden in them. He is then instructed to run his fingers through his hair if he has any and to pull down his ears to let the officer see behind them. The inmate is then told to open his mouth, so the officer can see, and run his fingers around the inside to make sure no contraband is concealed there. He then raises his arms above his head so his armpits can be seen. At this point the inmate is told to remove his undershorts and lift his penis, then lift his testicles, again making sure no contraband is hidden there. He is then directed to turn around and raise his feet backwards showing the sole, one at a time, and told to wiggle his toes, to determine the absence of contraband. The last part involves the officer telling the inmate, still naked, to bend over and show his anus to the frisking officer. If no string is hanging out, a string is sometimes connected to a balloon filled with contraband, or no shine from Vaseline can be seen, this indicates the need to lubricate contraband to fit inside the anus, can be seen in there, then the inmate is told to get dressed.

One day after a visit, I strip frisked Tupac, something that was my job on many occasions. During the frisk, we were making small talk, something we did a lot. Even though this type of frisk is a serious part of any officer's job, as you can imagine it is a bit uncomfortable for both parties involved. Many of the most stressful situations inside prison are met with levity from staff and sometimes inmates alike. Tupac was pointing to his scars and I can attest to the fact that they were real and looked like they were left by bullets. In prison, I've seen a lot of bullet scars on the bodies of inmates. Tupac's were legit. I watched an interview on television where someone tried to say that Tupac faked the shooting and that he wasn't actually shot. Not true. Tupac told me they were from when he was shot in Manhattan. He pointed out three scars, two on his head, one on his hand and I said, "I thought you got shot five times?"

"I was. I got shot twice here too," pulling his undershorts down far enough to expose the bullet holes in his groin area.

"Oh shit," I thought to myself; that had to hurt. I then told him "Okay, take your undershorts off. Okay, now lift your penis" and he did. I then said, "Okay, now lift your testicles." He stood there for a few seconds just giving me a funny look, he must have been thinking if he should say it and then broke out in a full tooth smile and said "Mr. C... do me a favor. Tell your fuckin' homeboy CO's that I got two nuts." He then lifted both of them laughing and he started singing AC/DC's song "Big Balls" well his version of it "I have big balls. I have big balls. And I have the biggest balls of them all." Then he declared "they keep callin me, fuckin, one nut." He was laughing, but I sensed the teasing by the officers bothered him; officers can be relentless when teasing someone, both with other COs and with inmates.

This was the only time Tupac ever asked me for a favor. And as far as I know, he never asked any staff at Clinton for any special treatment.

I worked at least every four consecutive weekends because I had a rotating schedule that gave me every fifth and sixth weekend off. It was always my job to escort Tupac back to E-block. After a few weeks of escorting him, I asked him "why don't you request APPU? After all, in PC you only get an hour a day out of your cell and you get no programs whereas in APPU you're out of your cell most of the day, just like general pop and you can go to school or take wood shop or whatever."

"I never heard of APPU. Shit, my lawyer never said nuthin' about it. I'm gonna ask him what's up with that? Thanks, Mr. C."

"No problem," I responded. "You'll like the change."

On the walk back to his cell that day, I also asked about some of the people that he dated. Madonna's name came up. "What's Madonna like?" I asked.

"You mean 'M'? That's what her friends call her. She's cool and all, but she ain't like you think. It's all about persona, about the hype, publicity you know" he said "smoke and mirrors, image. She's like really fuckin submissive, you know? Not dominant like the media makes her out to be." He giggled, "You know what I mean, Mr. C.?" He opened his eyes as wide as he could. "But she drove me crazy, always wanting my permission to do shit. One morning she woke me up in bed and said, 'Pac can I go for a run?' She jogged and shit. I said, 'I don't give a fuck what you do woman.'" He gave a funny look, "I ain't her Master." He laughed. A rumor circulated inside the walls during the time he was at Clinton that Madonna had visited, but that is false. She never did visit Tupac. Another rumor that was spread inside the prison during Tupac's incarceration was that Salt-N-Pepa (an American hip-hop group popular at the time) had visited him. That's not true either.

"What about Janet Jackson?" I asked. Now he had my interest peaked. "Didn't you do a movie, *Poetic Justice*, with her?"

"Yeah," he replied. "She's pretty hot."

"You guys like friends and shit?" I asked.

"Friends? Uhm. Nah. But she did ask me to hang out with her after shooting was done one day. I went to her place, you know. She had like maids and butlers and a personal chef that lived with her and shit. I thought that was cool, but I didn't like the way she treated her help. And all she fuckin' wanted to do was talk about her. Do you think I'm pretty? Blah, blah, blah, she's smoking hot, but I didn't want to fuckin' talk about her."

"So… you a real gangster and shit? Your music is called gangster rap."

"No… I ain't like that. That ain't me, Mr. C., it's my image. I am what the public thinks I am. If it sells records, then that is what I am. I'm a chameleon. Business, you know. It's all about the Benjamins. It's all about the green baybe, I mean I ain't a gangster. Hell, I don't belong to no gang. The CO's here walk around like they are fuckin tough guys. You guys are more like gangsters than I am."

"Well, some of the old-timers here are pretty tough, but those guys don't say much. The guys with the S, for Superman, on their chests, well most of those guys just bark a lot." I laughed. "You're probably right, we could be the largest gang in New York State if we wanted. There are over 20,000 of us here. We do all stick together and the Blue bastards do always win. At least that's what it says in the CO's bathroom written in magic marker on the stall wall. We do have a code of silence that we live by; nobody likes a rat, not even a CO. And last, we are family. Even the ones not re-lated by blood are considered our Brothers. So, I guess we are like a gang, no, more like the Mafia" I puffed out my chest and started to laugh.

"Well then, you're a thug though; your tattoo says Thug Life," I said.

Tupac responded, "It's a cool tattoo, right? But it doesn't mean what you and a lot of other people think. It represents 'The Hate U Give Little Infants Fucks Everyone."

"Wow," I thought. "That's pretty deep."

"I ain't no thug though, Mr. C., not really. You see me, I'm just like you. I mean I grew up on the streets and shit you know with thugs for sure but I ain't a bad guy. The things I did in the streets were like a rite of passage. Like a white kid joining the Boy Scouts." Tupac laughed or at least he tried to, putting his hand up to his mouth and swaying his head slowly back and forth. It looked like his eyes were filling with tears and he was fighting to hold them back, his chin began to quiver and then just like that he was able to regain control "I didn't have a Dad and shit, so...."

I looked at him and, in that moment, I felt real empathy. "You didn't have a Dad?"

"Nope, don't even know who he is. My Mom's told me that there were three men in her life at that time and could have been any one of them. I don't want to know that bum ass nigga anyway.

The thugs on the street were my role models. They passed on their wisdom to me like a dad would. These guys are like — my brothers. The street thugs are my family. Family is family. You know about that right?"

"Yeah, I guess." It was obvious to me that he was remembering memories that made him uncomfortable so I said, "well what about the tattoo of Nefertiti? What's that all about?"

Tupac pointed to the tattoo on his chest, "This?"

"Yes," I said.

"Nefertiti was a beautiful African queen, a woman warrior like my Mom."

"Okay... I get it. That tattoo is your version of Mom and the heart symbol that has been overused for decades. I like it when you do that. Take something that is trite and make it breathe again, like a Phoenix from the ashes." He didn't disagree with what I said. He just smiled. "I heard you got keep locked for dirty urine?" Inmates are drug tested and disciplined by being kept locked, meaning confined to their cell for twenty-three hours a day for a specified period of time, if found guilty after a hearing. "What's up with that?" I asked. "You been smoking weed?"

"One of your homies that did my hearing and found me guilty said I was but it wasn't me." Tee Hee... Tupac gave that laugh that he did. It was distinctive. "Second-hand smoke, yup, smoke must have drifted in my cell from somewhere on the company, some other lucky guy was smoking that shit, for real."

"I saw your file. It says you're a habitual marijuana user."

"No, Mr. C. I gave that shit up. I swear to God. I'm tellin' ya." His eyes opened wide and wider until he smiled and broke out laughing.

I knew he was lying. He was telling me what he thought I wanted to hear, and I said, "good answer."

A few weeks later, Tupac was moved from protective custody to APPU and now my contact with him was multiplied many times. I would learn a great deal more about him in a short period of time. He was assigned a program in the school Monday through Friday, where I was in charge of that area. He was a teacher's aide helping the other inmate students with their GED studies. Well, his title was aide but when I always made my security rounds looking in each classroom to make sure there were no problems. He was always standing at the chalkboard teaching. The Civilian teacher usually had his feet on the desk with a cup of coffee in one hand and a paperback book in the other. I would look in the classroom through the window on the door and Tupac would see me and smile and throw me a peace sign.

The inmates in the school area got scheduled breaks like in public schools on the outside and when Tupac got his break, he would routinely stop by my desk on his way to the break room where all the inmates from his class went. He would ask what was up and I would usually start talking to him for a few minutes as long as things in the area were quiet and I had no other duties. One day I told him that he was more like the teacher than the teacher and he smiled and said "for real, right? Ain't that some shit. I only got a tenth-grade education, never graduated, and here I am teaching inmates, only in fuckin' America." He put his right hand on his heart, kicked his feet together, and began reciting "The Pledge of Allegiance" all the while making faces and laughing.

"I didn't know you didn't graduate. You seem pretty smart to me. Then again, I was talking to the college English professor that works here. He used to be a military intelligence officer and also once taught at West Point and he told me that a college degree isn't the only measure of a person's intelligence. Not by any stretch of the imagination. It's a piece of paper that says you attended and participated in all the required courses of college. He said he gives a "C" if the person shows up and does the homework correctly. He also told me some of the smartest people that he ever met had no degree." I told Tupac that I had always felt that a college diploma didn't necessarily make a person smarter than a person without a degree. Tupac responded by moving quickly up and down, standing in place, and throwing his pointer finger forward, and said "exactly… Damn Mr. C."

"I went to Baltimore School for the Arts when I lived in Maryland. Cool school," Tupac said, "my Moms sent me there. Best part of my life. I liked it, you know? Some crazy ass smart and talented people were there. That's where I met my girl, Jada Pinkett — she's my heart, for real, love of my life, you know, Mr. C? The one you carry here (pounding lightly with his right hand closed on the left side of his chest) But I moved."

"Oh yeah, I know. For me it was more like the song Frankie Valli sang, "My Eyes Adored You." Boy meets girl. Boy has crush on girl but because one of her friends liked him, he never dates her. What if, right?" "Yeah…" "Frankie who?" Tupac giggled and then hung his head and said "Yeah"… I sensed this subject was a serious one for Tupac because he was almost perfectly still, something he had a hard time doing. I could hear it in his voice. It was subdued and not playful. He was very respectful talking about Jada, never using a single word of profanity, and that look in his eyes, like the look someone has when they are at a funeral home, looking inside the casket of someone they dearly loved for one last time.

"I read she's with Will Smith?" I looked over at Tupac. "She's his girl now right?"

His voice changed as he answered, "He don't own her Mr. C."

"All I mean is he's with her. He seems like a cool guy, you know. Just my opinion," I said. "I've seen him on interviews on

TV and he seems down to earth, genuine kind of guy you would want to hang out with."

"He ain't." Tupac's face changed. His jaw tightened, "hype, smoke, and mirrors."

As we were talking, an inmate walked by us doing a little sashay and waved to Tupac with fluttering fingers. "Hi Pac," the inmate walking by us said in a very, very high voice. "I think that one likes you" I nudged my chin up toward the inmate walking by as I told Tupac.

"I ain't down like that Mr. C., hell no... hell no" he started talking with his hands and he started rising up, almost standing on his tiptoes "I like women. I'm a freak for women. I mean, I really like women. No, I l-o-v-e women for real. One of those," pointing to the inmate walking by "lives on the tier above me and she, I mean he, whatever, keeps telling me to put my head down by the toilet. He wants to talk to me via the throne phone, by putting his head in the toilet and yelling to me. That's some crazy ass shit. I don't put my head near a toilet, in a toilet, or put my anything in any hole in this place. He said he wanted to give me some tomato soup or some shit. I yelled up and said I didn't want anything he had."

"Good thing you didn't take the soup. In here, if you borrow from another inmate, the price is two for one on your next commissary buy. And if he doesn't charge you, well, then you might have to barter with him if you have cigarettes or stamps and if you don't have those, well I'm sure you have something that he wants." I started to laugh and said, "It could have been worse; at least he didn't hand you his soap dish. One time I knew an officer who had to frisk a cell of an inmate that acted just like that guy after he was taken to the hospital. Anyway, this guy, girl, whatever, didn't like his penis and testicles so he decided to play doctor. He put his dick and balls on the metal bed frame and used a can top to cut them all the way off; might have been a tomato soup can top, I don't know. The officer said he found them in the guy's soap dish and that they looked like two grapes and a cocktail wiener."

I watched Tupac squirm like a worm and quickly grab his genitals and squeeze, making the most painful face and salt-in-an-open-wound sound that he could. He then said, "Mr. C. that's fucked up."

"Yes, true story," I said. "I'm not so sure about yours though, but if that's your story, stick to it." I was laughing so hard tears were rolling down my face.

Chapter III

Getting to Know Tupac

The more I talked to him, the more I began to like him, and I felt like I wanted to get to know Tupac more. So I went home and bought his CD, "Me Against the World." I listened to it, and I must admit I didn't really like most of it, but I liked the song "Dear Mama." It said something to me. It struck a chord. It felt real. The very next day after I listened to his music, I saw him in the school area on his break and I called him over to my desk.

"You know I listened to your new album" I said.

"Did you like it?" He said and bent over toward me, smiled, and waited patiently, looking deep and directly into my eyes, as if giving me a lie detector test looking for any signs of untruth. "I mean, did you really like it?" I could see that he was growing impatient waiting for the answer.

"Kind of," I didn't want to hurt his feelings with a bad review, but I wasn't going to lie either. "It's really not my thing, too much violence, too much hate. I really liked the song about your Mom though. You ever think about getting away from the gangster shit, killing cops, shit like that, and mellowing the rhymes out. It's working for LL Cool J and Dre?"

"Not you too, Mr. C.," Tupac dropped his arms down to his sides in obvious disappointment and in a little louder voice than he usually used said, "Damn. You almost sound like those bitches Dolores Tucker and Bob Dole. They don't like my rhymes either. They be all trippin', acting crazy, wantin' to kill rap and shit. Suffocate it."

"Chill, relax, I'm just saying. Maybe try to mellow it out a bit. Appeal to the greater masses. The women buy a lot of records or get their boyfriends to do it. That's all I'm saying."

"Don't sweat it, I'm cool." Tupac said as his guard came down. "You aren't the only officer to tell me to change my shit. Some old guy told me to try country."

I looked at him and started laughing. "Now that's funny."

As I was saying it, Tupac said, "can you see me doing country?" Then he started to line dance and sing 'Achy Breaky Heart' by Billy Ray Cyrus.

"Stick to Rapping," I said, and Tupac burst into laughter. Maybe he was a great Rapper but his voice wasn't suited for singing, at least I didn't think so, and he wasn't good at playing basketball either. The other inmates assumed he was good at it because of his role in the movie *Above the Rim*, even though he didn't really play any basketball in the film and were asking him to play. He told me he couldn't play "b-ball," what the inmates called basketball, a lick, he sucked at it, and he didn't know what that myth was all about but he couldn't jump either. When he told me this, another inmate was standing next to him and said, "you got that right."

One day a white inmate with carrot top red hair and freckles was walking with Tupac as he was coming down the hallway. I had noticed that Tupac sometimes hung out with this guy and I also knew that this white inmate bragged to the officers that they could never catch him with dirty urine. I once asked him how he was getting over on the staff and he told me that he was a constant drinker of copious amounts of water. He said he was never without a drinking cup to get water from the drinking fountain. He also said that his kidneys were in a constant state of evacuation. Inmates are allowed to drink all the water they want. So, I had asked the drug test officer if it was possible and he said he didn't believe it, but I think that inmate was telling the truth. I also noticed that since Tupac started housing in APPU he wasn't coming up with dirty urine. Maybe it was just that he quit smoking dope or maybe his new friend was schooling him on how to beat the system.

So, when I saw Tupac walking with the red head, I couldn't resist to say something jokingly to him, "careful that guy you're

with has a bad reputation as an outlaw." The white inmate immediately quipped "that's right, I can't lie. I am an outlaw. What did
my parents expect? They named me Jesse James." The inmate continued talking with Tupac and me for a few minutes. He told us
that when he was little other kids used to pick on him on the
school bus because he looked like Alfred E. Neuman on the cover
of Mad Magazine and they would take his lunch money. And I
must admit that he kind of did resemble Alfred E. Neuman, even
as an adult. Anyway, he went on to tell us that he got tired of the
kids bullying him and he decided not to let it happen anymore.
He said he went home and filled his metal Scooby-Doo lunch box
with rocks, Duck taped it shut, and then he took one of those ri-
diculously big Souvenir pencils and sharpened the end of it. The
next morning, he got on the bus and sat in the back where he always did, where the Bus driver could never see him. But this time
when the bullies asked for his lunch money, he defiantly told
them no. He said that one of the kids went to hit him but this time
he hit the kid in the face with his lunch box and stabbed him in
the leg with his giant pencil. "Wow," I said and looked over at
Tupac, who started laughing and asked him, "What you in here
for?" The inmate looked square at Tupac and smirked "robbery."

One day Tupac stopped by my desk and I had spoken to him
quite a bit by now so I figured what the hell, I'll ask him, "what
about the crime you are in for? Did you do it?" After all, he was
talking to me a lot now.

"They gave me one and a half to four and a half Mr. C., one and a half to four and a half for something I didn't do. They said I raped this girl. I ain't gotta rape nobody. Nobody. Girls be giving me shit, begging me to fuck 'em. I fucked her, that girl. I did. But she wanted me to. It was consensual. Me and my homies had fucked her before. She was a freak. That night she said she wanted to fuck me again, and I said what about my boys? Yeah, sure, she told me. So, I took her to the bedroom and got busy, you know. When I was done, I sent her out of the bedroom and told the homies they could have her. Then she started buggin', you know, acting crazy and shit. She was crying in a chair. I asked her what's wrong and she said she changed her mind and shit. All I did was try to talk her into doing it. That's it. She ran outta the hotel room and into the hallway crying and shit and someone saw her there."

"That's it?" I looked at him in disbelief. Of course, almost every inmate in prison is innocent. Just ask them. "It's like this," Tupac went on to say "if someone is threatening to jump off a roof and you tell them. Go ahead. Jump mutha' fucker and they do; you are guilty of coercion. I grabbed her ass and told her what a freak she was you know? But I was just trying to change her mind. They charged me with like eighteen charges, but they convicted me on the two felony counts of first-degree sexual abuse. I touched her, yes, but she was the same girl I just fucked a few minutes earlier. Ain't that some shit, I beat the rape charge cause I didn't do it. She admitted on the stand that she wanted to have sex with me. I didn't rape her. But still... there will always be people that think I did. That some bullshit. You think if that was anybody else that shit would have happened? I fought the law Mr. C. and they won; know what I'm sayin'? I'm a fuckin' thorn in their side. Judge wouldn't even look at me during the trial. Justice, what justice? I was guilty before I walked into the room."

Tupac was bitter, but if what he said was true, who wouldn't be? Sometimes venting frustrations helps inmates in prison. It doesn't change anything, but it makes them feel better just to have someone listen to their side of the story. This train of thought is the reason why New York State adopted a Grievance system after the Attica Riot of 1971. Grievances are not about their crimes but about anything that occurs inside the prison that they feel is unfair. Grievances don't usually change anything but gives the pressure cooker of prison a way to release some steam.

After Tupac told me his version of the details of his crime, I figured that he was comfortable enough with me to discuss almost any topic. He liked to talk a lot, and so did I, so the words came fast when having conversations with him. Sometimes I could barely keep up with what he was saying because he went off on tangents, something I am prone to also. I could tell that he was intelligent and articulate. His hands were always in motion, adding to his speech. He actually had a lot of charisma. The conversations with him were never dull. We talked about everything and nothing, about living and dying and life. We pondered why are we here? Do we have a purpose? Not the type of conversations that I was able to have with many people.

We both agreed that we liked philosophy. He told me he considered Shakespeare a great philosopher and that he liked his work. One of his favorites was 'Romeo and Juliet'. He also liked Aristotle and Plato, and he liked Socrates, who is credited as being the father of western philosophy. I told him I didn't care for Shakespeare but 'Romeo and Juliet' was probably the exception; most of his stuff reminded me of reading law journals, very dry and way too formal for me. But Aristotle and Plato were pretty cool. And I liked Socrates, especially the quote that has been attributed to him over the years where he said, "when the debate is over, slander becomes the tool of the loser." Socrates was ahead of his time and his words still ring true in modern politics, in prison, and in life. In Tupac's case, it was his enemies that felt they were losing the debate and had begun a smear campaign against him while he was in prison. I told Tupac that it's the things like quotes and deeds of greater people than me that make me wonder and think. If it stirs emotions inside me or creates thought outside the box, then I probably like it. I found it interesting that someone the world had given the moniker of thug and gangster clearly was highly intelligent and articulate. I found it interesting that the author that Tupac was stoked about reading at the time was Niccolò Machiavelli, and his famous book titled, *The Prince*. The book was originally printed in 1532 about the conduct of men in power and the principles they governed by. He told me that I had to read it. "It was Da bomb."

Tupac told me he loved everything about this book, especially the part where Machiavelli says, "to fool one's enemies, fake one's death." Tupac loved this quote but the quote that he chose to show me from the book was the one that said "it must be understood... that a prince... cannot observe all of those virtues for which men are reputed good, because it is often necessary to act against mercy, against faith, against humanity, against frankness, against religion in order to preserve the state... he must stick to the good so long as he can, but being compelled by necessity, he must be ready to take the way of evil...."

I doubt Tupac wanted me to see him as an evil person but rather to see him as a person that was capable of doing evil; a malady shared by the entire spectrum of colors of the whole human race. I also believe that he wanted to impress upon me that he was intelligent and that, although he spoke and wrote in average diction, he was anything but average. His messages were universal.

The new lifetime Moniker of criminal didn't seem to bother Tupac on the surface, but the idea that he would be remembered as a man connected to a sexual crime did seem to fester deep inside him. I would have had to have been blind not to see that he had a genuine appetite for knowledge and he was open to reading just about anything and everything. But the work of Machiavelli and his book *The Prince*, because it dealt with how to attain political power through fear, how to get what you want regardless of how you get it and, most importantly, how to own it, was fascinating to him. I think the quote from *The Prince* that sums it up best for how Tupac felt was this, "it is necessary for a Prince wishing to hold his own to know how to do wrong."

I told Tupac, "Machiavelli sounds a lot like a crime boss."

Tupac responded, "Mr. C. you're not going to fuckin' believe this but I met 'John Gotti,' you know... the big dog, boss of the Gambino crime family. Say hello to my little friend shit." Pac pretended like he was shooting an imaginary machine gun. "I was at a club in Manhattan one night and these really big white dudes grabbed me and pulled my black ass out to the alley where there was a van. They blindfolded me and told me to shut the fuck up. They weren't going to hurt me. Their boss wanted to see me. I ain't gonna lie, I thought I was gonna shit myself. I asked who's your boss? They told me to shut up again and said I would find out soon enough. When they removed the blindfold, I was standing before John fuckin' Gotti himself. We were at some kinda secret club and shit somewhere, I don't know where, but there was gambling, drinking, and lots of women, beautiful women."

I responded to Tupac, "When I was at Sing Sing prison back in the eighties, I went to New York City around September I think, and they closed off Mulberry and Canal Street for some kind of Italian block party. I was told then that the whole thing was paid for by Gotti. The people in the city loved him like Chicago loved Al Capone. Why would the Godfather want to meet a young rapper like you? You're cool and all, but what can you do for him? After all, nuthin for nuthin that's what the mafia always says. They do you a favor and you owe them one."

"Gotti wanted to discuss business. A proposition he had for me."

"What kind of proposition?"

"You know I can't tell you that Mr. C., shit. You know the code. And you know the penalty." He-he, Tupac started laughing. "Swear to God Mr. C., for real. Word, I ain't lyin."

I have often wondered about that conversation. Gotti went to prison in 1992 and Tupac was up and coming in 1991; he was famous but not nearly as famous back then, so what Gotti wanted with him is anyone's guess. I did believe him though, that he met the Don. Two things that Tupac did have in common with John Gotti was that Gotti also did time at Clinton Prison back in the mid-1970s and he was also considered just another street thug by the officers.

"Ok, I hear ya," he wasn't going to talk anymore about that and I knew it. "Back to this guy Machiavelli. I've never read or even heard of him but the quotes are cool." They seemed pretty deep and Tupac knew that I liked that kind of writing. "I've read a few books lately too. This one by Joe Hyams called *Zen in the Martial*

Arts is pretty cool. I like that quote in it that says 'A man who has attained mastery of an art reveals it in his every action' — Samurai Maximum. Now that's deep. Hyam's talks a lot about Bruce Lee, and I like Bruce Lee."

"Yeah, me too," Tupac said and then does his verbal imitation of Bruce Lee, Whaaaa!!! "He was dedicated, intense. He's the greatest that ever lived."

"Yes, I agree. Bruce Lee used to say a lot of cool stuff, one time he said, 'Become the water. If you pour the water in the pot become the pot.' So, I guess that applies to people too," I said. "If you want to understand another person you have to become the other person, right?"

"Bruce Lee also said, 'If you love life, don't waste time, for time is what life is made up of.' I really like that. I guess he never wasted any time, not a minute. He hungered for knowledge and perfection. He wanted to know and do everything." These qualities reminded me of Tupac.

I guess Tupac took what I said literally because a few days later I had to go to Lower-H block for something, which I seldom did. I was on number one company, which was where he lived. His cell was number 25. As I walked by his cell, I was about to stop and talk for a second. When I approached him, he was sitting on his stainless-steel toilet facing me with a big unlit cigar in his mouth, because smoking inside your cell was not allowed. He was just sitting there with this 'your mind is in another place look.' He had a pen in one hand and a piece of yellow legal paper in the other hand, apparently writing something while doing his business.

I said, "Whoa, sorry." I quickly began to continue down the tier. Not what I was expecting to see, although not uncommon. I remember looking straight ahead and seeing little pieces of mirrors sticking out of a few cells facing toward the entrance so that they could see anyone entering the gallery. "Walkin" one of the inmates inside their cells yelled out; this is how the inmates tell other inmates that an officer is walking on the company. This way the inmates can stop whatever unauthorized behavior they are doing, like smoking weed, making shanks, or whatever. I didn't smell anything unusual or see anything unauthorized going on that day, and I just kept walking when I heard a familiar voice. "Hey Mr. C., come on back. It's cool. I'm just takin a shit." I remember thinking that most inmates would have reacted with some kind of negativity, usually profanity of some kind because of the intrusion into their privacy even though in prison there is no real privacy. This basic right we take for granted is stripped away the minute a person is convicted of a crime. Inmates while inside their cells are always subject to random security observations by staff during the course of their duties such as security rounds or for suspicion of unsanctioned activities. The only real exception is that only a male officer can observe a male inmate or a female officer for a female inmate, in any intimate setting. Anyway, I reluctantly returned to the front of his cell and acknowledged him, all the while a little uncomfortable. I interacted with him with some small talk but honestly I don't even remember the conversation after that episode.

I do remember thinking that Tupac was practicing the same philosophy as Bruce Lee. He wasn't wasting any of his time. He was writing that day and I saw him write more times than I can count. Seems he was always writing. Years after his death I watched an interview on TV where he said that he didn't write any songs while he was in jail. I guess he didn't want anyone to think that he was somehow inspired by anything related to his incarceration. I understand that. But I'm not so sure that he didn't write anything in prison. One time in the visiting room he told his visitors that he was working on a song and started rapping it. I told him that he couldn't rap in the visiting room and he responded to me by saying, "You got that, Mr. C." He always gave me respect.

After I told him about the Zen book, I said "I also read a cool book of poetry recently."

Tupac interjected, "Poetry is my thing. I like to read it and write it. Maya Angelou is one of my favorites. I got to meet her. What a great lady."

"That's cool," I said "I've read a little bit of her stuff. I like her. But the poetry I really like is written by this guy Paul Laurence Dunbar. I read his book *It's a Lowly Life*. You ever read anything by him?"

"Hell yeah," Tupac's eyes opened up wide, and he said, "that's my shit. You know who Paul Laurence Dunbar was?"

"Yeah," I answered, "he was a poet that was an elevator boy. He wrote poetry in the late eighteen and early nineteen hundreds."

"He was way more than that Mr. C. He broke the fuckin' chains. He was like the first African-American recognized around the whole fuckin' world. Mutha' fuckers called him sir and shit. He was recognized by whites. Damn, Mr. C., what you know about a black poet?"

"You should know me enough by now to know I don't care about all that shit. I care about what he says and how he says it. I don't care about the color of his skin." I reached in my desk drawer and pulled out Dunbar's book (Dodd, Mead and Company, 1903) and opened it to show him a poem. "This is my favorite."

Life

A crust of bread and a corner to sleep in

A minute to smile and hour to weep in,

A pint of joy to a peck of trouble,

And never a laugh but the moans come double;

And that is life!

Tupac said, "Yeah, that shit is dope. I like that shit too. Damn, Mr. C."

"I don't read everything, but I read what I like," I said, "and I like movies too if they have a purpose. You know? One of my favorites is the old black and white movie *It's a Wonderful Life* by Frank Capra."

"Hell Mr. C.," Tupac interjected, "I like that one too."

I told him, "Well my friends disagree because they say it's too shallow, not complex enough. I think it's complicated and deep. I mean, think about it, if we're not born then the story would have to be rewritten. Nothing we create would be created by us, nothing we say would ever be heard, we would never share our thoughts with the world and we would not be mourned or remembered by anyone because we would have never existed. Our lives, our words, our deeds are as important as seeds are to trees. As insignificant as they may sometimes feel our lives impact and inspire others in ways we may never know."

"Yes. Yes. Yes." Tupac said "That's it, the bomb. You blew that shit up, for real. You sure you're from these mountains, Mr. C.?"

It seemed to me that we saw many things alike even though we were from very different worlds. He was from the inner city where people didn't tend to trust strangers because people were getting robbed and killed on the streets. I was from a small town where we didn't lock our cars or our house doors at night; my Mom had always told me that locks only keep honest people out. But the biggest difference was that he was an inmate and I was an officer. To him, it probably at first was because he was black and I was white. To me, it made no difference. Still, to me, it was undeniable that we shared views that mirrored each other. We were both convinced that nothing in this existence we call life happens by chance and that everything is predestined. Everything, the day we are born and the day we die, and everything in between. Our meeting was supposed to happen. He survived being shot five times on November 30th, 1994, so that we would meet. We both believed that for whatever reason we met and that there is some kind of purpose and in time it will reveal itself.

One day we had a conversation about intelligence. We both agreed that intelligent women are attractive, at least on an intellectual level. And we discussed that we both liked intelligent people in general and that sometimes they were hard to find in prison and even outside in the streets. We also agreed that in groups of people like parties or whatever we sought out interesting people to talk to.

I told Tupac, "I heard somewhere that Bill Gates likes to immerse himself with smart people and that makes sense to me. After all, if you are the smartest person in a room or at a party or whatever, then all the people conversing with you are drawing from your experiences or your intellect. You gain nothing of substance from the experience, but if you socialize with people smarter than you, then you draw from them and in turn become a little smarter or wiser for having done so."

"Damn Mr. C., I pretty much do that shit already," Tupac said "but I think the real shit is the intelligent people that can go to any person no matter who you are talking to and talk to them on their level, you know. I can talk to a guy on the street or I can talk to a guy with a Ph.D."

I had to agree with him. It takes a certain level of intellect for someone to mimic their audience. It was also evident to me that Tupac was the smarter of the two of us and I was definitely gaining something from our talks.

I added, "the only exception to seeking out people smarter than ourselves I think is that we seek out people or knowledge that has something to contribute to us on some other level. It can be anything really. It can be as simple as how someone treats others like Mother Teresa did that inspire us or admiring the creations of others like Van Gogh, Monet, or Picasso that might spark our imaginations."

Tupac said, "you killed that shit, Mr. C." He was always saying stuff like that. He was always complimentary. Another favorite topic for both of us was our dreams. Not what we would do in life but what we saw when we slept at night.

I told him my dreams were in color and that they were quite vivid, and I many times remembered them. He told me that his dreams were also in color and vivid and that he too remembered them. I told him that I write poems, stories, and articles, whatever. He told me that he wrote a lot too. Sometimes I told him when I get an idea while driving a car, I frantically search for something to write on, sometimes a napkin, anything really. Sometimes in the middle of the night, I jump out of bed and my wife will ask me what's wrong, and I tell her nothing I'm looking for a piece of paper and a pen to write whatever thought came in my head before I forget it. I like to write, and it seems like fiction for me almost writes itself. It plays like a movie in my head. I just write whatever I see playing. Tupac said he knew exactly what I meant.

"Well," I said, "everybody thinks and dreams and writes that way, right?"

"No," he said. "Not everybody. We do. You're blessed, gifted by the man upstairs Homie" pointing up with his finger.

"Yeah right," I was laughing, thinking that he was joking with me or patronizing me. I didn't know, but who wouldn't like to hear that they were something special? So, the talk continued. "What about precognition? Do you believe in it?"

"Hell yeah, damn — Mr. C., there's a lot more inside your book than your cookie-cutter CO cover."

Tupac had experienced a couple of precognitive dreams he said that had come to pass. I told him that I had experienced a few too. I said, "for me, they were really personal, and no matter how much you wanted to change them." Tupac interjected at the same time as I was about to say it, "you can't." "Exactly," I said. "We are merely spectators. We know the ending of the movie before we see it but we can't give it an alternate ending."

"Yup," Tupac shook his head up and down fast. "Damn."

"Pac," I said, "I had a cousin tell me a story about a guy he knew on an Air Force base. He had a dream about a plane crash the night before he was supposed to go on a mission that required him to fly in a plane. He was so upset by the dream that he called in sick that day. That morning since he wasn't working, he decided to go to the Base Exchange or the BX as it's commonly referred to, a type of retail store for military personnel. He pulls into the parking lot, coincidentally, at the exact same time as the plane that he should have been on ascends overhead. When the plane flies above him the engine falls to the earth striking him. He and all on board the plane that he was supposed to be aboard were killed, regardless of his futile efforts to change his fate."

"Damn Mr. C., that's some weird shit." Tupac then told me that he had an aunt who lived in the south, in one of the Carolina's, but unfortunately, I don't remember which he told me. Anyway, he said she read tea leaves, and that she read palms. She told him that he had a short life-line on his palm and that she saw darkness in his future. I asked him what the darkness was that she told him that she saw, but all he told me was that whatever it was, it was bad. I think he believed his aunt and that he had a feeling he was short for this world. He didn't fear death or if he did, he didn't show it. It appeared to me that he knew it would happen while he was still young but didn't know exactly when. And he gave me the impression that he always wanted to do everything a hundred and twenty percent so that he would be remembered. I think the same way Charlie "Lucky" Luciano, a famous mafia gangster in the 1930s did when he said, "I never wanted to be a crumb. If I had to be a crumb, I'd rather be dead." Lucky Luciano also did time at Clinton. It was told to me, early in my career, that he donated several expensive items to the construction of the Catholic Church of St. Dismas — "church of the good thief" — that is located inside the walls of the prison; listed on both state and national registers of historical buildings. I often wondered to myself if Luciano thought his money could buy his redemption.

Tupac's conviction of a sex crime was not a reality that he had any control over and by now I was realizing that he wanted control over every aspect of his life. If he didn't have this control, it seemed to me that it was like strapping him into a straightjacket and telling him to relax and accept it. He told me he was not guilty of the crime he was convicted of but that the Government wanted to destroy him. This is not the first time an inmate told me a similar story. In the unit where Tupac was housed, there was another inmate that was convicted of sex crimes. He also happened to be a teacher's aide in the same classroom as Tupac and they regularly spoke to one another. This inmate also told me that he was innocent. He claimed that he didn't do the crimes he was accused of and that he was about to blow the whistle on the government for their involvement in illegal activities with other countries like running weapons and drugs to support new regimes to overthrow the ones they didn't like when he was charged. He said our government was part of 'A New World Order'. He would regularly say that there are only a handful of people in the world that are really in charge and they are called the Illuminati.

The inmate that shared the title of teacher's aide with Tupac, I remember vividly. He regularly had adult stress acne on his forehead that looked like a mild case of chickenpox. But what I remember most was how adamant he was about the government and how if they want to discredit anything you say then all they have to do is get someone to accuse you of a sex crime. If you get convicted then anything you say is a lie and if you beat the charges then someone will always think you did it and got away with it, and again they won't believe anything you have to say. This inmate was a former decorated soldier and agent of the Government. If any of what he said was true, then the Government had underestimated charging Tupac with a sex crime because if there was any breath left in him, I don't think they could have stifled his voice.

Tupac seemed like he wanted the world's embrace and universal accolades for all his endeavors and I think he thought that acting not only let him walk in the shoes of anyone but that it could let him open the door to everyone's house and become a part of their family, loved by everyone, not only Rappers. When he told me the names of the movies, he acted in, it was if he was telling me the names of his own children. He told me, "My life changed Mr. C. when I acted in the movie named, *Nothing but Trouble*, I knew this was the shit that I could love, then it was *Juice and Poetic Justice*, and I really liked *Above the Rim*. You ever see any of my movies Mr. C.?"

I told him, "not yet, but I'll probably check them out later."

He replied, "That's not all I've done, I got a few more movies that I'm going to be in Mr. C." His excitement ramped up a few notches. "I got one that we just wrapped up called *Bullet* and then I'm working on one called *Gridlock'd*, but the one that's really dope is *Gang Related*. I'm gonna act with Jim Belushi. You know, John Belushi's brother? That mutha' fucker is funny."

"Yeah, I know who he is. That's cool. I like Belushi's stuff. He is funny."

"This movie ain't gonna be a comedy though. Check this shit out Mr. C. I'm going to be Belushi's partner and we gonna be dirty cops. Police. Yep, Police" Tupac laughed. "Imagine that shit I'm gonna play an officer of the law. I get to be one of them. Ha, ha. I want to do more acting and win an Academy award and someday I want to direct and write my own movies."

"That's cool," I said, and I remember thinking, wow, he has done quite a bit. Tupac was probably more famous than I thought. Something that he was always telling me was that life is a circle. He was always putting his hands together, forming a circle and telling me that a circle has no beginning and no end. Basically, he told me that what you throw out into the universe goes out, and boomerangs back to you threefold.

"Everything happens in threes, Mr. C.," he said. "Three is a number from the Egyptians. It represents faith, wisdom, and courage. A lot of things in life are represented by three. Think about it, Mr. C., birth, life, and death, you know, past, present, and future, all threes."

"A Psychic once told me that my number in this life is three," I said, "so that is pretty cool." I agreed with Tupac about the circle which I saw as Karma. And I will admit that I didn't think that Tupac was an angel, so Karma might not be his friend, but then again, he never proclaimed to be an angel either. In fact, he told me just the opposite that he did a lot of bad things in his life, but when I would press him to elaborate, he would always plead the fifth. The Fifth Amendment guarantees due process to refuse to incriminate oneself so he wouldn't elaborate. It didn't surprise me he was a street guy, and he was street smart. In prison, there is a saying that snitches get stitches, and I didn't see any razor blade scars on his body from getting cut. So, I guess I'll never know what he meant.

He said, "when all my shit comes back to me, I'm in trouble. You can't fight destiny, right Mr. C.?" Tee Hee. He laughed. "I guess I'll just have to keep my head up and my chest out and handle it. That's what I always do." It seems like he accepted everything and anything life dealt him. He was always in good spirits, considering where he was, at least on the outside.

While we were on the topic of Karma and God's divine plan, I couldn't help but think about the cross that was tattooed on his back. He had a lot of tattoos, but this one was hard to miss. It was big, taking up most of his back. It reminded me of a Greek Orthodox or Gothic cross, or maybe a combination of the two. Tupac was very creative and the idea that a Gothic cross usually has a circle in the center and his had what looked like a square in the center. He loved circles, so why not put the circle? But putting the box in the middle might represent thinking outside the box. I didn't ask him. I was too busy trying to wrap my head around a gangster rapper with a giant cross permanently inked on his body. He had other tattoos too, quite a few actually, but this one looked religious, I thought.

So, I asked him, "You religious? I'm curious, you one of those religious gangster rappers knocking on doors and shit?" Ha ha. I laughed.

"I believe in God, Mr. C. Probably the same one as you. I ain't no Bible thumper but I believe. You think cause I'm here I might find a different God? Doesn't everybody round here find God when they come to prison? I ain't Muslim if that's what you're asking, but the inmates here are trying to convert me to the chosen five percent. I told them if Allah magically transports me out of this place then I'll convert." Ha-ha. Tupac laughed.

"I believe in God and I pray to him every night even though I'm here. Maybe God is teachin' me something like in Milton's Paradise Lost. (John Milton, English poet 1608-1674.) Where man was like Adam, you know, Adam and Eve? And he disobeyed God and God teaches him a lesson of obedience and shit. I had it all. You know? But must be a reason I'm here, you know? If you haven't read it, you should, it's deep. Hell, I don't think you gotta to go to church just to believe in God. It's not about how much money you give to them, the Priest, Reverend, or whatever. It's about what you do for the next nigga. Know what I mean? Church is about money. That's all they care about, a bunch of fuckin' hypocrites. Catholics, Mr. C., are like the biggest criminal organization in the fuckin' world. Back in the day when the conquistador Cortez conquered Mexico, he brought missionaries from the Catholic Church with him. These missionaries would make you convert or tie you naked to a whippin' post and whip your ass till you died or you converted. Then they stole those poor mutha' fuckers' gold. Sent it back to the Pope and decorated their churches and shit. The Catholics are the richest religion on earth. Now if that don't sound like a mob. That's mob shit."

"Really..., I didn't know that, I'm Catholic." Not really what you want to hear but I knew Tupac was pretty smart. So, I did some research later and found that he was right about how the missionaries converted so many Mexicans to Christianity. "I think I understand, not going to church doesn't make you a bad person. Some of the wickedest people I've ever known sit in a pew, pray, and put money in the collection basket and think they have bought a ticket to paradise. I know that for centuries men have fought wars they call Holy and killed their fellow man in the name of God. Yet still, I believe in God. And I agree with you that you don't have to go to church on Sunday to talk to him or for him to hear you, but what about heaven and hell? Do you believe in them?"

"Yeah, next life shit. I believe. Bible says God judges. Not one man or one woman on this earth can judge me. Just remember God hates sin but loves a sinner. It's between me and him. He knows." He made a face. Tee-hee. "Don't matter I'm doing my time. I'm already in hell. Some of these officers think I'm fuckin scum. They judge me. They think they're God. I figure that if the real God wants me to suffer for my sins, then he put me in the right fuckin place. No offense, Mr. C."

"Well, prison is a world inside a world," I said. "Nothing inside prison is normal. Society doesn't want to know what goes on in here. You think all officers are pieces of shit and the officers think you and all inmates are pieces of shit. Doing time in prison is like surviving in a war. You fight the battle as long as you can and if you're lucky you someday leave the war but it doesn't leave you. It burns deep down like the oil fires in Iraq. I've seen inmates assault officers and I've seen officers assault inmates. I've seen inmates shit in a Styrofoam cup and throw it in an officer's faces for no reason other than that the officer happened to be in the wrong place at the wrong time. But the best part is the State's position that says that officers must refrain from any retaliation including beating them bloody when this happens, easier said than done. I'm not saying that I'm any different; I've wanted to hurt some of these guys too. I'm not going to lie. I'm going to tell you something. I don't usually talk about it. But I remember when I first started working inside the walls. I was young. One day, this odd, white inmate charged at me with a metal wastepaper basket and tried to hit me in the head with it. I threw him headfirst into a glass window. I was pissed. I thought he wanted to kill me. He blocked his face with his arm going through the window and shards of glass stuck out of his arm when I put his hands behind his back and put the handcuffs on him. I remember going to the prison infirmary later to get checked out for any injuries and that same inmate was there, nearby in another room, on the operating table. Out of anger or curiosity, I don't know, I looked into the room and watched the Doctor sew him up. The inmate refused any shots to numb him and simply just stared at the bright over-head lamp. It appeared that he felt no pain — no pain. I couldn't believe that this piece of shit felt nothing. I guess this bothered me because that day on the way home I relived the incident in my head over and over again. When I got home, I never mentioned it to my wife. As a rule, I never discussed work at home with my family. That night I went to bed and my wife woke me up when she started screaming in the loudest, scariest, voice I've ever heard from her. My hands were around her neck and she was yelling over and over that her arm was hurting, that it hurt, so bad. She was standing there caressing her right arm, shaking, wincing with pain, the same arm that the inmate should have felt pain from ear-lier. I felt horrible. The only thing that I can figure is that I really wanted that scumbag to feel pain and he robbed me of that satis-faction. And somehow his pain transferred to her. It still gives me the creeps and yeah, I still apologize to her sometimes.

That is what prison does to the mind. It alters it. So yeah, offic-ers sometimes have attitudes toward inmates. Sometimes officers are able to move on for things they've seen or things that have happened to their friends who they consider their brothers but some have a hard time. I don't hate inmates or anyone for that matter but I'm not like everybody else. In war sometimes you develop a hate toward the enemy. I'm not saying it's right, Pac; I'm just keeping it real. You are right though. Prison is hell for both of us. I'm doing my time in here, just like you, only I do it in eight-hour shifts. At least you can accept where you are and settle in. I live in one world and work in another."

"Mr. C.," Tupac said, "you're cool so I'm going to keep it real with you. I ain't afraid of the devil. I'm not. I ain't afraid of his posse or his hell when I die, I told them to burn my ass. I ain't gonna feel it."

"You want to be cremated?" I asked.

"Yup, told my homies to burn me, crispy, you know the way I like my wings, and take my black ashes and put me in a blunt with some good shit and party with me."

"Now that's fucked up," I said and just shook my head.

Chapter IV

The Visit Room

October 2, 1995, I watched the trial of the century on TV. It concluded with O.J. Simpson being acquitted. I couldn't wait to go back in to work and ask Tupac what he thought of the verdict. And I finally did see him after his visit concluded on that Saturday. I asked, "think he did it?" I was curious to see what his answer would be, thinking he might say innocent because of his racial sentiments when he first arrived in Clinton. "What do you think?"

Tupac cocked his head back and returned the question back, asking me to tell him first what I thought.

"I think he did it – but I think the police were afraid that O.J. might get off because he was a celebrity. So, I think they took the glove from the crime scene and planted it at O.J.'s Rockingham Ave. house to tie him to the murder. Only it backfired. I've seen it in law enforcement where the belief is that the end justifies the means. If they think someone is guilty, they don't care how they prove them guilty because as far as they are concerned the accused deserves it. So, what about you? Did he do it?"

"Hell yeah, he's as guilty as hell. If I was him, I would wear a bulletproof vest and hire a lot of bodyguards and shit cause mutha' fuckers want to kill his ass. He killed a white girl." He chuckled. "You know Johnny Cochran is on my payroll, right?"

"No, I didn't know that."

"I got him on retainer. If he can get O.J. off, he oughta be able to get my black ass outta this place."

One time I asked him, "What do you miss the most about being free?"

Tupac looked at me and turned his head to the side thinking and then said, "a long, long, hot, fuckin' shower Mr. C., swear to God. I ain't gonna lie. A lot of stinky ass mutha' fuckers in here."

"Well," I said "the state doesn't want you to sue them for getting scalded with hot water," I laughed, "at least it's only those fuckers' asses that stink. There was an inmate here a few years ago the officers called ass-face. This guy always took his shower the same way. He would turn the shower on steaming hot, lather up his washcloth with soap, wash his left arm, then his right arm, bend over, wash his left leg, then his right. He would rinse. Then, like clockwork, he would lather up his washcloth again, scrub under his testicles, wash his penis and reach around to his ass where he thoroughly cleaned it, smiling from ear to ear he immediately went to his face with the washcloth and generously washed it."

"That's some funny ass shit, Mr. C."

"I'm surprised that it's the shower that you miss the most," I said.

"Well, I do miss women. I mean, I love women; I love everything about them. The way they look. The way they smell, damn Mr. C., you're killin' me. That's probably why I didn't say it. I'm trying not to think about it." He giggled.

Tupac used to tell me a lot that he really liked my name. And for some reason, he really liked the way it sounded. He said it was dope. He thought there was money to be made in merchandising it. He said like a character's name or a product name. I said, "Thanks." I didn't know what to say. Twenty-plus years later, my name has been used for everything from publishing, cologne, designers, movie characters, and much more. I guess he probably did really like my name but he was also a pretty smooth talker too. He seemed to know just what to say to people. It was like he had read the book, *How to Win Friends and Influence People*, a 1936 book by Dale Carnegie about interpersonal skills.

I liked Shakur's first name, and I asked him if the name Tupac meant anything.

He responded, "yeah it's African — means Warrior's son."

I thought he said rising sun and asked him, "What about the sun?"

"No, not sun, son," Tupac laughed. "Warrior's son."

"Oh. Yeah, that's cool" I said. "It's a good black soldier's name, right Mr. C?"

"Not bad," I said. I sometimes wonder why he told me that is what his name meant because I saw an interview with his Mom and she said his name meant shining serpent. Maybe he didn't want to tell me that he was named after a snake but liked his African definition better. Or maybe his Mom did tell him when he was young that he was a Warrior's son. I don't know. I think I like Tupac's version. After all, I think it fits him. He told me that his Mom had been a Black Panther in the early 1970s, so it didn't surprise me that he was very proud of his black heritage. When he told me, he arched his back and took a deep breath, and wore it like a Purple Heart on his chest.

A lot of my interaction with Tupac was on the weekends during visits. I always sat at an old elevated wooden desk with a slanted top about two feet or so away from Pac's table. It was a small square one like in a cafe that could seat four people. I sat elevated high enough as to give me a Hawk's eye view of the entire room. Tupac was always smiling and laughing. He was like a child in a man's body. His laugh reminded me of Michael Jackson's, very high-pitched. He was always kidding around with the other inmates and always asked me when he arrived for his visit if I wanted him to sit in Police, he pronounced it in syllables, Square One, the moniker he gave the visiting table closest to my desk. My Supervisor had given me instructions to keep a very close eye on Tupac and not let other inmates or their visitors interact with him. The facility was concerned Tupac might create chaos in the visiting room from people's fascination and curiosity with his celebrity.

Tupac sometimes expressed to me that he felt like George Bailey because so many of his so-called friends acted like they didn't know who he was when he went to prison. He told me that he didn't need them anyway. "Sometimes, Mr. C.," he said "it's hard to tell who your real friends are. Everyone says they're your friend, smokes a blunt with you, spends your money, wants to hang out with you, but they're just frontin', bum ass freaks and frauds, smoke and fuckin mirrors. It's hard to recognize wolves in a dark room when they sleep with sheep." I could tell by his sharp words that it cut him deep.

His aunt Yaasmyn, he called her his aunt. I'm not sure if they were actually related but she was one person that never left his side. I could tell he was very close to her. She was a regular visitor but usually only visited on weekdays. She was from New Jersey and the officers nicknamed her Big Bird after the character on Sesame Street because she was really tall and walked hunched over. She appeared to be his secretary, bringing a folder with account balances and a writing pad and things like that. Tupac would hold court, where he was the judge, at least that's what the officers called it when his Aunt and several of his cousins would all sit across from him and wait for his instructions. I remember one day I stopped by the visiting room on a weekday and Tupac was on a visit with his aunt and a few other guys. One of the guys visiting told him that he needed money to fix his car. Tupac told him that he gave him money last month for that. I remember he laughed but I think he gave it to him anyway. Tupac appeared to me to be quite generous with his family.

Tupac's Mom, Afeni Shakur, visited a few times on the week-days also. I did not see her, but the officer in charge of the visiting room when she came told me that Tupac would become engaged in arguments with her often. I always thought it might be over money. Tupac gave his Mom two houses; one of them was located in Georgia, a place he said he loved, and money to live on. At least that is what he told me. After talking to the visiting room officer, he told me that the gist of the disagreements was over him becoming too much like her. She was always telling him that his mouth would get him in trouble. She told him something about paying a high price for her choices and she didn't want the same for him. She told him to use his brain and make money. Everything in this world requires money for him to achieve his dreams. She told him knowledge is power.

One of the most frequent visitors was Keisha Morris. Tupac was always excited like a child that just drank two cups of Cappuccino when she came to visit. I always remember this one day she came to visit when she and Tupac arrived at the visiting room at the same time. They were both at my desk checking in. I wrote down who they were and told them where to sit. Tupac introduced her to me as his fiancée and went on to tell me what great shape she was in. "She does like a thousand sit-ups a day, Mr. C., look at that body," pointing to Keisha. "D-a-m-n," he said putting his hand up to his mouth and biting, "show Mr. C. your abs." She shook her head and said in a low stern voice, "no." She looked straight at him with this dirty look.

Tupac said "Do it. Come on. P-l-e-a-s-e?" He fluttered his exceptionally long eyelashes at her and she melted. I saw a few women while he was there reacting the same way when he said please that way, drawing it out, and batting his long lashes at them. Keisha raised her shirt just enough for me to see her sculpted abdominal muscles. I was impressed. Not only was she in awesome shape but Keisha was a very pretty woman. She always dressed to the nine and often wore high heels which gave her a little more height because she was short but the heels looked very becoming on her. Tupac had a good eye for the pretty ladies. He was also very proud of the fact that she was attending John Jay College of Criminal Justice in New York City at the time.

Whenever Keisha came to visit, she and Tupac had their own little routine. The first thing he did was send her to the vending machines. Only visitors can buy from the machines because inmates can't possess money. So, Keisha had to get his barbeque chicken wings and a can of Orange Crush soda. He would tell her to hurry up and get out there to get his wings before the machine sold out of them. Sometimes the vending company would only fill the machines once a day and he loved his Orange soda and wings. But he only liked the wings if they were burnt, really burnt. He would send Keisha back to the microwave at least twice and sometimes more saying, "I told you I like my shit burnt." He would laugh.

Not long after Tupac arrived at Clinton, he married Keisha, on April 29, 1995. I was working that day. An officer escorted Tupac into another room adjacent to the visiting room where Keisha, dressed in a pretty beige dress, wearing high heels and with her hair done, wearing it up, was waiting for him. There was a female local Justice of the Peace from Dannemora waiting inside for them. The whole ceremony lasted only a few minutes. They returned to the visit room, and I said, "Congratulations." They both seemed quite happy that day and after the visit, Tupac was so excited that he had a hard time containing himself, "now I can get a trailer visit," he said to me like a child on Christmas Eve that couldn't wait until Christmas day so he could open his presents. Conjugal visits did regularly happen at Clinton where inmates could spend a few days in a private trailer unsupervised with their wife and have sex. But Tupac never did get approved for that kind of visit.

A few weeks after the wedding, a woman arrived at the facility that was not on Tupac's visiting list. Usually, the visitors are approved in advance of the visit. The front gate called me and asked what I wanted to do.

I called lower H-block, the APPU housing unit where Tupac lived and had someone ask him if he wanted to visit with this person. He did. He was called down to the visiting room and this young, very attractive Hawaiian-looking woman greeted him. She told him that she was a huge fan and that she found out that he was locked up here at Clinton, so she drove from Syracuse, New York, by herself, to visit him. He thanked her. They both sat down at the table. Shakur then looked at me and stuck his hand in his mouth and bit down, smiling. He couldn't take his eyes off her breasts and it was obvious from where I was sitting. She was blessed in that area. The two of them were laughing and joking. Then Keisha walked into the room, and the room got quieter as she approached my desk.

"Who is... that woman... with my husband?" Keisha asked with that feline look in her eyes.

"A fan, I think. You will have to ask him," I said.

And she did. "Who is this woman?" She clenched her teeth.

"She's a fan of mine," Tupac beamed. And then he introduced her to Keisha. She didn't look happy. They all sat down and started talking. Tupac started looking at the girl's breasts again in front of his wife and she gave him a hard elbow to the chest. "Damn girl," he blurted out loud enough that others in the room looked over at their table. Ordinarily, I would have warned her that she couldn't do that and if it happened again, I would request to terminate the visit, but I didn't say anything to her. I guess I thought he had it coming.

Tupac would tell me that day after the visit that he recently bought two black 750 IL BMW cars, one for him and one for Keisha. He also said that he gave Keisha five hundred dollars a day allowance to spend and that she l-o-v-e-d to shop. His marriage to Keisha Morris was brief. It didn't officially end until 1996, but she stopped visiting him about three months after it began. I never asked him why it ended, but the abundance of women writing him and visiting him unexpectedly, and the fact that he couldn't get approved for a trailer visit surely didn't help.

Without missing a beat, a new girl started visiting Pac; her name was Desiree. I remember that she had a tattoo on the upper part of her arm that read, "Go ask Tupac." I thought that was funny because whenever Tupac would get up to go to the bathroom and leave the table, other visitors would lean over from visiting tables next to them and say can you get me an autograph from Tupac? Talking between visitors and inmates on different tables is not allowed and I would have said something to them the first time it happened, but I didn't have to say anything because apparently this girl knew the rules and wasn't going to screw it up or she didn't want to share Tupac with anyone. She would quickly pull up her shirt sleeve and reveal the tattoo with a bit of an attitude. I thought to myself, I like this girl. She doesn't take any shit.

One day the band Digital Underground came to visit. Tupac was a member of the band before he went solo. It was where his career took off. They had a hit called "The Humpty Dance." He was also in the movie, *Nothing but Trouble* when they performed in the flick. The movie included Chevy Chase, Dan Aykroyd, John Candy, and Demi Moore. I watched the movie. It was pretty good. The leader of the band "Shock G" aka Greg Jacobs also known as Humpty Hump seemed to be a good friend and I think Tupac's like for him was genuine. I remember the group was talking about cars, and Jacobs told them he had the same Toyota 4Runner for eight years. He said he didn't need a new one. He liked that one. I remember Tupac being all animated like an excited child when he was reminiscing with the group about a trip they had taken together. I think it was somewhere tropical and they all rented mini bikes. He told them they should do that shit again.

On one weekend it was Jasmine Guy who visited Tupac. She was the actress that played Whitley on *A Different World*, a sitcom with Jada Pinkett that ran from 1987 to 1993. She was a very petite attractive woman. On his album *Me Against the World* it talks about Tupac getting shot and signing himself out of the hospital against his doctor's wishes. It says that he was staying at a safe, undisclosed location. Tupac told me that he stayed with his long-time friend Jasmine Guy, and here she was. I remember that while visiting she arrived at the prison in a black tank top and the officers at the front gate wouldn't let her visit until she got another shirt to wear over it. Shirts without sleeves aren't allowed in the visiting room to avoid intentional or unintentional views of breasts of both men and women. Most visitors would have been upset by this rule because it was a hot day and the visiting room was stuffy, but Ms. Guy was a true lady and accepted the rule graciously. Tupac requested to take a picture with Jasmine, which was granted, and I escorted them to the room for photos.

On the way back a young, chubby, little boy around nine or ten tapped Jasmine on the leg as she walked by him in the hallway. "Excuse me. Excuse me," the little boy said sheepishly.

"Yes," she replied.

"Are you Jasmine Guy?"

"Yes."

"Can I have your autograph?"

"Sure, do you have a piece of paper?" She asked.

"Yup," he said as he grabbed a piece of scrap paper from his pocket and handed it to her. She signed it and he thanked her and left.

As we were walking back, I leaned over to her and said in a low voice, "Why didn't you tell him no?"

"Aww... I couldn't do that" she smiled and laughed softly.

Tupac bragged to me that Jasmine Guy read more books than anyone else he had ever met. And Tupac himself was a sponge. He read a lot. But he was impressed with her. "She even reads while she flies and always has a paperback in her purse," he told me. His respect for her was blatant.

A few days after the visit, I was under investigation. Someone said that I had the photo of Tupac and Jasmine Guy together. I didn't, but I knew who did. My area Sergeant asked me if I took the photo from Tupac. I said "no."

"An inmate said he saw you take it from him. I am going to interview Shakur," the Sergeant got serious, "and if he says you took it, you will be in a lot of trouble."

"Go ahead, ask him. I didn't do it."

The Sergeant called for Tupac to be escorted to his office to interview him in private. He later told me that when the Sergeant asked him if I did it, he said no. He said the Sergeant pressured him more, trying to get him to say that I did it until Tupac interrupted him and asked, "Why is it you are asking me about the officer that treats me like a human being, and never ask me about the ones that treat me like a piece of shit?" The Sergeant looked at him with a stone face. He gave no answer. He simply just ended the interview and sent Tupac back to his cell.

I was standing there that day when the photo was taken. The photographs are taken by an inmate worker with an instant camera. When the photo is pulled from the camera, the photographer waves it a few times for it to dry all the way. He then usually gives it to the inmate to take with him. That day the officer assigned to supervise the room told the photographer to hand him the picture. "I'll take that," he snatched the picture and put it in his shirt pocket.

"Tupac asked, "can I get another picture then?"

"You're done," the officer pointed to me and said, "get him outta here." The officer that really did take the photo happened to have a brother who was a Lieutenant there. That same brother later became the Superintendent of Clinton Correctional Facility.

Of all the things that took place in the visit room probably the most historic thing I witnessed was when Tupac got a visit from Marion "Suge" Knight, CEO of Death Row Records, along with the record label's lawyer, David Kenner, who I remember clearly because he had a white stripe in his hair. Tupac was already on a visit with Desiree when Suge arrived. What surprised me was that usually whenever I see people on television, they always seem bigger to me than when I see them in person. Jasmine Guy looked

taller on TV than when I met her. She was very short, but Suge
Knight, well he was a different story. He was an ex-football player
and I knew that, and I've seen many men bulk up and body build
in prison, but honestly, Suge was the biggest guy I had ever seen.
His shoulders were four feet apart at least. He stood six feet plus,
bald head, neatly dressed in fresh blue jeans and a bright red shirt,
with a neatly groomed beard. He and Kenner walked up to my
desk and stood silent before me with a blank expression. Before I
could say anything to them, Pac jumped up from his visiting table
and met them at the desk. I just looked up at Suge and thought...
holy shit. Tupac was anxious to introduce him to me. He kept
jumping up and down like a kid waiting for an ice cream cone.

Tupac blurted out, "Mr. C., this is Suge Knight. His record label
is Death Row. West coast... baby. He wants to sign me."

I said, "Cool." I was thinking to myself that I was just starting
to hear about Death Row and Suge Knight on MTV. Tupac then
told Suge, "shake Mr. C.'s hand. He's a good man." I remember
the look on Suge's face. It was a look of utter disgust. It felt as if
he hated me or thought I was beneath him like I was a beggar in
the streets asking him for money. I felt his vibe. It was that strong.
Tupac told him again to shake my hand and insisted that he do it.
Suge took his time in defiance but did finally concede. He slowly
took my hand and shook it. I couldn't wait for the shake to be

over, it was almost painful, definitely beyond firm. It was like putting my hand in a vise and turning it a few times. It was evident that Suge really wanted to sign Tupac on his label.

The three of them sat down, Shakur, Knight, and Kenner, at the table. It was funny to see Suge sit on the chair at the table. He looked like he was sitting on a little child's chair in school. He was that big. About an hour or so later, Tupac came back to my desk grinning from ear to ear carrying a few loose pieces of paper. He showed me a handwritten contract. It was between Tupac and Death Row records for what he said was four point seven five million dollars. "They are going to give me one point four million dollars for my bail and the rest after I give them three albums. What do you think?"

"Sounds cool," I said. "Congratulations."

"Thanks." He was beyond happy, clicking his fingers, swinging his arms back and forth doing a dance all the way back to the table. It was funny. Suge even cracked a smile.

After the visit, when all the visitors were gone, I told Pac, "looks like you're gonna be rich again."

"Money ain't all that, Mr. C. Anyone that has ever had any kinda real money can tell you that only people that don't got none think it will make them happy. I ain't happy. I'm here, my life sucks for real. This money is bail. That's it. Ever since I got money, I got problems. Everybody, I mean everybody, they all be suing me. Everybody wants a piece of my ass." Tupac grabbed his own ass and laughed. "Pretty soon I ain't gonna have an ass left. Shit, God damn."

"Just be careful," I warned him "you might have just sold your soul to the devil."

"Like Robert Johnson did, Mr. C.?" Tupac asked. Johnson was a famous blues musician from Mississippi that Faustian myth says that he sold his soul to the devil at the crossroads in exchange for his musical talent.

"Yup, like Robert Johnson did, and someday the devil may ask for your part of the bargain," I told him with a serious look.

"Shit, I ain't afraid of no devil. If it gets me outta here, then I'll give him whatever he wants. I'd rather break bread with the devil than have that fuckin' guy above me ask me one more time if I want tomato soup." He started laughing. We both laughed. "For real Mr. C., I gotta get out of this place. It feels like a fuckin fishbowl. Everybody that walks by this room stops and peeks in at me. Officers stop. Visitors in the next room are always looking in through the door when it opens. Even other inmates are always looking at me. I'm a fuckin goldfish. I don't belong here."

"I hear ya," I said, "you are a goldfish. You're trapped, everybody pisses on you and the world sees you covered in urine." I silently empathized to myself. He was always being stared at, talked about, and whispered about, loved or hated, everybody had an opinion about him.

"Exactly," Tupac said "you surprise me. You understand a lot. That's good, empathy, empathy, empathy. Always put yourself in another man's shoes. Do that and you'll strike gold, drink Dom Perignon (champagne) and shit, nine hundred a bottle. Smoke Cubans (cigars) like me. But just remember, careful what you wish for, you might just get it."

"I don't think so. I can't rap."

"Write a book," Pac said "why not? Write about prison. Write what you know, but make sure that if you do write something that you protect it. I used to write stuff and then send it to myself in the mail because it's a Federal entity."

"Huh" I said.

"Yeah, go to the Post Office and certify the mail that has your writing in it, send it to yourself, and when it arrives back to you don't open it. We used to call that the "Poor Man's Copyright.""

"That's a cool idea. I never thought of that. The date is on the envelope and it's stamped by the Government. Maybe… someday, I might do that. I think it was Ernest Hemingway that said in order to be a man you should write a book. Maybe I'll do it. I have thought about it, but I've always believed that everything happens when it's supposed to, so we'll see." Tupac did drop a seed that day that for decades would remain dormant. I guess he was right I had seen a lot in prison. I had many stories inside my head.

Like I said earlier, a lot happens in the visiting room. It is, after all, one of the most interesting places inside the walls, I think. A place where the outside world comes to see the best side of the inmate's personality that they have to offer, even if for most inmates it isn't always real. A place where Tupac was on a visit one Saturday and a boy, two or three years old, still in diapers, was sitting facing him, sitting on his father's lap, who was also an inmate. Visitors always face each other and inmates always face each other when sitting in the visit room. I remember Pac kept watching the little guy. He would bob his head up and down and side to side just outside the kid's view and then reappear and stretch his mouth and stick out his tongue, making weird faces. The boy responded with belly laughs and smiles. It was amusing and heart-warming to watch. It never got out of hand and was innocent, so I let it continue throughout the day. At the end of the visit, I asked him if he had any kids and he told me no. I said, "are you sure?"

He laughed and said, "I'm sure. I double wrap. A.I.D.S. and STD's you know?"

"Don't you want a little Tupac?" I asked.

"I can't take care of myself, Mr. C. Look at where I'm at. This world is fucked up. Not a place to bring kids into."

I figured he might tell me that he wanted at least one, but that day he was adamant that at that point in his life there weren't any plans for a little one. I then told him that I was going to tell him a little story. He rolled his eyes and giggled. I guess he knew it was going to be another prison story; I did like to tell them. "A few years earlier," I said, "I remember a little man about seven or eight years old that came to see his father in the Pop visit room across the hall. He spent most of the time sitting on his Dad's lap. He had a smile on his face that stretched from one ear to the other. His cheeks must have hurt at the end of that day. I watched him as his Mom told him to hug his daddy goodbye. He wrapped his little arms around his neck like a Boa constrictor. His Mom told him to let him go so they could leave. He refused. He held on so long and so tight his father had to pry him off. The father told the boy to do what his momma says. The boy said, 'No, I don't want to leave. I want to stay here with you.' The inmate bent down and looked his son squarely in his eyes. 'You can't stay here in prison. It's for bad people. I killed a man, son. I belong here, you don't.' The little boy began to cry. 'I'll kill a man and then I can stay with you, Daddy.' At that point his father raised his voice and put his open hand out as if he were going to spank him and said, 'go with your momma or I'll beat your ass. You hear me. Go. Get out of here.' The boy's mother yanked him up and carried him out. He kicked and screamed the whole way out of the visiting room. I watched that inmate, a killer, cry like a baby after his son left the room. Maybe that's when I realized there are two sides to every man, even though that inmate was not someone I particularly liked very much. He always walked around like a tough guy, a Blood gang member." I looked at Tupac and said, "I don't know why you don't want kids, it's none of my business, but I get it." Prison is no place to be a father. Unless you're visiting your son. I don't think I'll ever forget that day. The day Tupac met his father. It's still fresh. One day a visitor named Bill Garland showed up to visit Pac. Not too long before his release. The visit went normal. They both sat down and talked for a while, laughing and seemingly enjoying each other's company. On that particular day, the noise level in the room was louder than usual and I didn't really hear any of what they said. But at the end of the visiting hours, when the visitors were asked to leave and the inmates stayed in the room, Tupac approached the desk and pointed to Mr. Garland, who kept looking back as he exited.

I remember Tupac standing there with big puppy dog eyes, struggling to get the words out of his mouth, holding back the tears that were quickly filling his eyes. "You know who that is Mr. C.?"

"No."

"That's my Dad." His words cracked. He was shaking his head, slowly. I guess he was letting it all sink in. But saying it in such a way that I felt like he was proud to say it. Maybe he finally felt like he found his identity, like he belonged.

I said, "I thought you told me that your Mom didn't know who your father was."

"That is... what she told me. But this dude said that he's my pops."

"And you believe him? I mean you are worth some Benjamins" I laughed.

"Yeah, I believe him. Don't I look like him?"

"Yeah, I guess I must admit you do." Tupac had some hair on his head during his stay at Clinton. He never shaved it that I can remember. He trusted the inmate Barber to cut his hair with clippers with a guard attached but he probably didn't trust another inmate with a disposable Bic razor to shave his head. On this occasion, I felt real empathy and I was happy for him. And he seemed happy too.

While at Clinton, Tupac wrote a screenplay in longhand called *Live 2 Tell*. He was very excited about it. It was based on his autobiography mostly. He told me it was like part fact, some fiction. He wanted the movie to start in Black and White with him as a young man running from the Police. It chronicled his youth and continued until the night he was shot five times in the lobby of a Manhattan recording studio called "Quad" in New York City and survived. He asked me to read it and tell him what I thought. It felt good that he wanted my opinion, but I never did read it. He said that he had just sold it to someone and that everything he touched turned to gold. He bragged to me that he could write something on a piece of shit and some mutha' fucker would want to buy it.

During a visit one weekend, I would overhear a conversation about the night he was shot that he was having with a couple of visitors. It went something like this, "that mutha' fucker Stretch was with me when those bum ass niggas walked up and shot my ass. I looked up and that turncoat mutha fucker was smilin'. Smilin'. Don't worry. I know, mutha fucker, I know."

I would later make a point to talk to Tupac in the school area about what I had heard. "Listen, Pac, you got to leave the situation with Stretch, alone. You're going to end up getting yourself killed with the gangster shit."

"Don't worry Mr. C. It's cool. I'm going to have me some body-guards, some bulletproof vests, and walkie-talkies and shit. Death Row's got my back. Suge ain't gonna let nothin' happen to me. West Coast baybe, West coast, West coast."

I looked at Tupac and said, "I thought you were from New York City?"

"Yeah," Tupac responded. "I was born there but my heart beats for Cali. I love that place."

I smiled at him and said, "Yes, but New York City is your where you met your homeboy Biggie, right?" Tupac's face became contorted and his voice changed, "that fat fuck. He's a piece of shit. I treated him like a brother. Let him spend the night on my couch when he didn't have a place to stay, and he turned on me like a street mutt. You like that fucker?"

I could feel the heat from Tupac like a blazing inferno and I didn't want to fan the flames, so I said, "Nah, I never listened to anything of his. I was just curious." I quickly changed the subject.

Chapter V

Bail

Just before Tupac was released on bail, I was in the restroom inside the facility and I remember the prison's Superintendent entering the bathroom and standing next to me at the urinal. An uncomfortable situation, I must admit, peeing next to the boss. He greeted me with a pleasant, "Hi Officer Christopher. How is everything going?"

"Good," I replied. "I guess we'll be losing your celebrity soon."

"First, we don't have any celebrities here." The boss said with conviction.

"Well," I said, "infamous then. Shakur told me that he will be going home soon on bail. He told me that Johnny Cochran is one of his attorneys."

The Superintendent started laughing, "That's a good one. I don't think even a dream team can get him out. I've been in Corrections for more than thirty years and I can't ever remember any inmate being released on bail from prison after they are convicted. You can't believe what inmates say."

And what the Superintendent said ordinarily would be true. Inmates lie. That's what they do but, not always. I don't think it was Johnny Cochran though, that really made the bail happen for Tupac. He was in jail for at least seven months before anything in the courts was moving in his favor. He never did tell me which lawyer made it happen only that it happened. I know it wasn't Suge, not directly anyway. Tupac, just before his release, was trying to find a way to raise bail that is what he told me and he wasn't too successful at finding people willing to be associated with him financially because of his crime. It was Death Row who stepped up at Pac's request and offered a contract and the money that he needed to post bail.

A few weeks before Tupac was granted bail an inmate who happened to be white and also happened to be in prison for a high-profile racial crime committed in the early 1990s in Long Island against a black kid told me that he had hooked Tupac up with his lawyer Alan Dershowitz. This kid had told me on more than one occasion that his crime was not racial, that he knew this black kid and they were friends but this kid stole a jacket and he and some other kids took it back by using a baseball bat. He also told me that he helped Tupac get a better lawyer. Usually, I would have said yeah, right, but I believed this kid. In my career, I had to make a lot of judgment calls on the validity of statements told to me by inmates. Sometimes part of it was based on the person telling me. This kid was mild-mannered, respectful, and showed no signs of violent behavior. He also spoke with a stutter and was small in stature. In my opinion, he was the furthest thing away from being a street thug but was closer to being an average unintimidating kid on the block and I took his words at the moment at face value.

While in prison Tupac didn't associate with many people, even though he could have had his pick of any type of inmate from bodybuilder, gang member, religious group member, to contract killer to hang out with for his protection or conversation, but he picked this kid. Protection in prison provided by other inmates is not allowed inside the facility but is sometimes covertly bought by the inmates with money, sex, or drugs. The best example I can remember was the common belief by the officers, although they could not prove it, that "Preppy Killer" Robert Chambers was an inmate that against Department of Corrections' rules employed the services of several white bikers that sometimes wore a colored handkerchief in their back pocket to identify their biker gang affiliations. Although displaying gang colors was not allowed the inmates found creative ways to display them. Several bikers were almost always seen shadowing Chambers in the yard and during movement in the hallways of the prison while he was at Clinton. The only difference was Chambers did his time at Clinton in Population and not protection.

Tupac must have also believed the white kid's story too because the kid's girlfriend used to ride with Tupac's wife to visit him during the time he was married. I believe, but I cannot say for certain, that the kid's lawyer, Alan Dershowitz, who represented O.J. Simpson and also represented Mike Tyson, was responsible, at least in part, for Tupac's petition with the New York State Court of Appeals that was heard and finally entertained. I read the decision by the Court of Appeals that affirmed the order to grant bail to Tupac Shakur and it states, "Although CPL 460.50 limits defendants to one application for bail pending appeal and Mr. Shakur was denied bail on his first attempt, the Court said his first application was a nullity because it was made before his notice of appeal was filed. Therefore, it said, his second application, on which bail was set at $1.4 million, was properly entertained." The acronym CPL represents Criminal Procedural Law.

Before Tupac left prison, he told me that he was friends with Mike Tyson. That Tyson was writing letters to him while he was at Clinton. Shakur was proud that the once heavyweight champion of the world was his friend. Tupac said, "Mike Tyson. Fuckin' Mike Tyson, Iron Mike, the heavyweight fuckin' champion of the world wants me to write a fuckin song for him. Can you believe that shit? Tyson's my man." Tupac began pretending to throw uppercut punches saying "one, two, one, two."

"Whoa… you can't do that. No boxing, no shadow boxing, no sparring, or any other forms of fighting including martial arts are allowed. Not even if you're just kidding around. Trying to get yourself in trouble?"

"Oops, sorry Mr. C., you got that." He started laughing. "It's hard for me not to get excited. Tyson is the man, the king."

"Alright" I said, "I get it, but you can't do the punching stuff." I knew it must have been hard for him. Asking Tupac not to talk without expressing what he was talking about with his hands was like asking a dog not to wag its tail.

"You know Mike Tyson is a pretty smart mutha' fucker, you know, maybe not like reading books and shit smart, but in living life, street smart. We're a lot alike. That dude's been through some shit, but you can't hold that nigga down. He's stronger than before he went to prison. Mike didn't have a dad either, you know. His Mom raised him. Tyson's the real shit."

Tupac talked a lot about Mike Tyson and how much he wanted to see him when he got out. I was curious if Tupac was friends with Tyson so I asked Tupac's correction counselor if Tyson was on Tupac's visiting list. Counselors help inmates with their sentences by doing reviews on their behavior while in prison for parole. They tell the inmate what programs they need to take while incarcerated and they also keep a list of people that are approved to visit the inmate such as friends and relatives. Tupac's counselor showed me Mike Tyson's name, address, and phone number as listed by Tupac. Tyson was approved to visit, but he never did visit Tupac at Clinton.

Tupac, according to articles I've read over the years, said he got to see Mike Tyson on September 7, 1996, at the MGM Grand Hotel in Las Vegas at Tyson's fight against Bruce Seldon, for the WBA (World Boxing Association) title. Tyson made his entrance to Tupac's song "Let'z Get It On." I'm sure that Tupac was on top of the world that night.

Whatever the truth was about what lawyer actually made the court entertain Tupac's request for bail, it was entertained on October 12, 1995, and Tupac Amaru Shakur walked out of Clinton Correctional Facility on bail — against all odds. A white limousine picked him up and drove him and a friend to the airport. A few days after his release, one of the officers was bragging about how he knew the chauffeur that drove Shakur that day. The driver told the officer that Tupac was handed the biggest blunt, which is a hollowed-out cigar filled with marijuana, he had ever seen by another passenger when he got in the car. They partied all the way, he said. Tupac told me that he gave that shit up, so I guess it couldn't have been true. Wink. Wink. But then again, maybe old habits are just too hard to break.

During one of the last conversations I had with Tupac before he left, I told him that I decided someday I was probably going to write that book. I told him it would be about our times together

OUT ON BAIL: TUPAC AND HIS PARTNER SYKE MOMENTS AFTER HIS RELEASE FROM THE CLINTON CORRECTIONAL FACILITY IN NEW YORK

in prison. I said, "I'll bet you someone will read it." And Tupac being Tupac encouraged me.

"You should do that shit Mr. C. just — keep it real. If my name is on it, then it will be a best seller. Just remember you need a hook to sell a book. I'm getting some celebrities and shit to read my books and write reviews. Someone should recommend it so others will want to read it." He looked at me like you would a child after you explain something to them, waiting for me to ask a question and when I didn't ask it, he began to laugh. That was one thing Tupac did a lot of in prison. Laugh. One of the things I remember most was that his laugh was contagious. He was always clowning around, cracking jokes, smiling, laughing, a playfulness to him that even prison couldn't kill. I guess it was just in his nature, like the class clown who wants to be liked. I couldn't help but ask myself if his thug image was just that, an image, an act. Maybe he was acting for his audience outside of prison, acting like his character Bishop in the movie *Juice*. I didn't see him as a real thug, and I've known more real thugs in prison than I can count. But rather I saw Tupac as a fragile and complex person who just wanted to be a corner piece in this perplexing puzzle we call life.

After Tupac's release from jail on bail, I remember the morning that I was reading the paper, something I did daily, and I came across an article about a rapper named Randy Walker, aka "Stretch." It said he was chased by a car and shot several times in a drive-by shooting, making his van bounce off a tree and hit a parked car; his car rolled over and killed him. The conversation that I had with Tupac came flooding back. Ironic, I thought, that his death occurred exactly one year from the day that he was with Tupac at Quad studios the night he was shot at almost the same moment, coincidence? Maybe, I half smiled as I thought it could be random, but then again, I also knew that the mob had an Old Italian saying that said revenge is a dish best served cold.

A short time after Tupac got out, I received a letter in the mail with a bogus return address on it. I don't know how he got my address but most officers' addresses aren't hard to obtain. Officers are often sued by inmates and they are always given the officer's addresses. When I opened it there was just a Polaroid photo inside; a prison polaroid photo of Tupac in his handwriting stating, 2 a good man Mr. Christopher, a reference to his respect for me as a person, see you at the crossroads, a reference to our conversation about him signing with Suge, West Coast all the way, a reference to his love for California. He said, I wish you all the success in the world and good luck on the book, a reference to our conversation about writing this book. And lastly, until next time, meaning either when he returned to prison or that someday he would see me again in this life or the next. I believe that he thought someday I'd write the book and he wanted me to have a hook for it. I have often thought that without this photo people will probably think that I was never liked by Tupac because he publicly said how much he hated corrections officers and all I have to say to this is — bullshit. I guess he probably said this for his thug image. He respected me and I respected him. Tupac gave me proof indelibly written in his own words on a picture taken while in prison and I have kept this picture all of these years since.

When his double album *All Eyes on Me* was released, I remember the inmates in Clinton were all bitching about it. They said Shakur sold them out for disco. The inmates incarcerated all thought his new material was too soft. At the same time, the white kid that was still at Clinton that was close to Tupac told me that Shakur told him that I was on a song he wrote but he didn't mention me by name. The inmate only said that it was something like,

'I met a man that thinks like me.' I don't know if he ever did release any song with words like that, but if Tupac said it, then he probably did.

About the first week in September 1996, I was working the school area and the same white kid again approached me and said Tupac sent a message with my girlfriend for you. Tupac said, "C U soon." I figured that his appeal was denied and that he was going to be sent back to Clinton to finish the remainder of his sentence, something I knew that Tupac would have dreaded more than anything. I thought I will get to see him again.

Chapter VI

The Man Behind The Curtain

I never did get to see Tupac again. On September 7, Tupac was shot in a drive-by shooting, and on September 13, 1996, I remember I was in my bedroom and I saw a special report come across the TV: Tupac Amaru Shakur dead at 25. I'm not going to say that it didn't affect me. I knew his injuries were critical, but I thought he'd pull through again, but he didn't. The news hit me like an uppercut from Iron Mike. I struggled to catch my breath. I remember thinking that he went out like Martin Luther King Jr. did, at the hands of a coward. I felt like the world lost another gifted person with so much to give and so little time to give it. It was the same feeling I had when I read the paper the morning of December 9, 1980. My body and my brain felt numb. I was in denial. This can't be true. John Lennon was shot dead last night December 8, outside the Dakota, in New York City. I only hope that Tupac will be remembered like John Lennon, for being someone that wanted to change the world. Someone who wanted peace but didn't fear war.

I will always remember Tupac. To me, he was the wizard, the man behind the curtain in *The Wizard of Oz*. Everything I saw on TV about him seemed to me an illusion. Smoke and mirrors, as he used to say. Tupac created a gangster persona and convinced the world that he was this larger-than-life figure. His confidence, his creativity, his empathy for his fellow man, and his charismatic personality was his recipe for his global success.

I still reflect on the day Tupac died. How I struggled to tell myself that he found his peace. We all know the speech, he's in a better place, blah, blah, blah. I was trying to coax my brain into calming down but my stomach wasn't listening. It felt like my body was trying to make a pretzel out of my intestines as I began to think back to the conversations that I had with Pac. Everything happens for a reason. And we both believed in precognition. It has crossed my mind that he knew he had a date with death but like he and I had discussed before I knew he couldn't change his fate. Reality is a bitch. But, God has a plan for all of us. We may not understand it but in his time we will, if not in this life, then in the next.

I am forever thankful for meeting Tupac Shakur. I believe that our paths crossed for a reason. He was part of my divine plan and I part of his. I am still reminded of 'George Bailey' when I think of him. His birth counted. His life counted. He had an impact on the world because he was born. My hope is that people will read this book and see a glimpse of the human being that I got to know and not the convicted felon and the negative rumors about Tupac that continue to persist.

I close with the words of a man I came to know as Pac, until next time — Peace Out.

Tupac Shakur

(A Poem by Michael Christopher)

Poetry primal in its' power fans an eternal flame

providing oxygen to ordinary words that bear his warrior name.

Your music still flies like a freedom flag, high with the masses, like
smoke from your ashes.

Your soul like your songs in our memory will live as long as the
Baobab tree.

Your hype like your Thug life imitated your art

when your body bleeding, barely breathing, lie riddled by bullets,
your lung ripped apart.

Déjà vu, another set of dark eyes looking straight at you, pistol attached to a familiar limb

Not the color of Birch but he was the color of you and you were the
color of him.

And so the world will remember your life like Seldon at the hands of
Iron Mike that night —

a short and unforgettable fight.

You were a Redwood that fell in a forest of mutes when like Icarus you
flew too close

to the sun. Your fame was your destiny, your fate, your undoing.

For the faithful fans keep your chins up, your chests out, and believe
  — that God has a plan.

You are another visionary whose words must not be erased because
  you are slain

this world may mourn your loss, it may feel your pain,

but it's the next world that raps and rejoices its' gain.

Your message will not be lost to the whiteness of pages never penned.

Fear not for in the end your words will be remembered in the
  company of good men —

spoken and taught with reverence like the messages of Kennedy and
  King.

HISTRIA BOOKS

PRENDE